Healing Made Simple:
Change Your Mind & Improve Your Health

Maggie & Nigel Percy

ISBN-13: 978-0692496978
ISBN-10: 0692496971

Sixth Sense Books
PO Box 617
Chino Valley, AZ 86323
www.sixthsensebooks.com

Table Of Contents

Chapter One - A Word Of Warning _ _ _ _ _ _ _ _ _ _ _ _ _ _ 9

Chapter Two - Why Healing Is Hard _ _ _ _ _ _ _ _ _ _ _ _ 11

Chapter Three - What Is Health To You? _ _ _ _ _ _ _ _ 39

Chapter Four - The Energy Body vs. The Physical Body 49

Chapter Five - Root Causes vs. Symptoms _ _ _ _ _ _ _ _ 53

Chapter Six - Make Intuition Part Of Your Healing Process
    61

Chapter Seven - Methods Don't Matter: Mindset Does 77

Chapter Eight - Intention Is Everything _ _ _ _ _ _ _ _ _ _ 93

Chapter Nine - Get Outside Help As Needed _ _ _ _ _ 107

Chapter Ten - Prevention _ _ _ _ _ _ _ _ _ _ _ _ _ _ _ _ _ 115

Chapter Eleven - The Healing Journey _ _ _ _ _ _ _ _ _ 121

Chapter Twelve - What Next? _ _ _ _ _ _ _ _ _ _ _ _ _ _ _ 129

Chapter Thirteen - Resources _ _ _ _ _ _ _ _ _ _ _ _ _ _ _ 131

Preface

In 1990, I was given a choice. I was still living a very conventional lifestyle, and I had health problems that the doctors were unable to resolve. My doctor told me that I would be better off accepting a prescription for Seldane and not worrying about trying to resolve the issue, which was too complex to deal with. He was saying I needed to settle for treating the symptoms and to give up on ever being healthy again.

If I hadn't had such a bad 2 years, I might have accepted his advice. But I had struggled with physical therapy for a knee injury that kept me crippled and unable to walk well. I had terrible digestive issues and broke out in hives no matter what I ate. My energy level was so low I could barely function. And I wasn't even 40 years old. He wanted me to give up.

I couldn't give up. I wanted to feel good again. In fact, I wanted to feel really good. I decided that my only choice was to take charge of my own health. I had two Biology degrees. I decided I could figure out something. I had no idea where that decision would lead.

Looking back, I realize that was a tall order, but I'd been living in pain a long time, and I was fed up. And that's what it takes for most of us; a level of pain so high that we refuse to tolerate it, that we MUST heal ourselves. So we do.

I spent a lot of time reading, studying and researching. What I discovered was that the allopathic viewpoint could not help me. Since I was living on the East coast, that was the main option I had. Fortunately, in 1994 I moved to Arizona, and a whole new world of healing opened for me. I began chiropractic, worked with a naturopath and started learning t'ai chi. I used herbs and supplements and even made my own remedies. I discovered a new way of looking at health. I became more focused on prevention;

more focused on creating health rather than fixing problems. I began to believe that I actually could choose to have good health for the first time in my life.

One by one, my symptoms began to disappear. It took years, but by 2000, I was healthier than I had ever been. I was doing Reiki and using flower essences and essential oils. Life was getting better every day.

Now at age 62, I am healthier still. I have more energy and fewer symptoms than at any time in my life. For someone who spent most of her childhood being sick, this is a real accomplishment.

What I learned along the way was that the conventional view on health isn't about creating health. It's about suppressing symptoms. It isn't about treating root causes. It's about getting rid of pain. I was sucked into that outlook for many years. It did not serve me well. I am convinced that if I had stayed in that mindset that I would be very unhealthy today. Instead, I took control of my health and learned how to create the health I desired.

I didn't make the choice to go down this path. It was made for me when my health was taken away from me. Like many others, I was forced onto a different path, a journey to healing that would totally change my outlook, my life and my health. Most of us don't change until the cosmic ton of bricks lands on us and ruins our health. Then we are willing to do anything to pick up the pieces. You know what I mean. You may have been there yourself.

This book is meant as a roadmap for those who would rather 'wake up' than have a ton of bricks flatten them. By making your choice before you lose your health, you will find the path much more fun to follow. But even if you've found this book after the bricks have landed, don't worry. It will help point you in the direction that took me years to find, so that you don't have to go through as much struggle, as many years of trial and error as I did. I wish you good fortune on your healing journey. It is my hope that this book will help it become smoother, more pleasant and a wonderful personal growth

opportunity for you.
Maggie Percy
May 16, 2015

CHAPTER ONE
A Word Of Warning

Warning

Healing and health are big topics. There are plenty of opinions on how you can become healthy. We don't pretend to have all the answers. We want to make it clear at the outset that this book is not about a healing method, so you're going to need to make some choices about healing methods along the way.

This book describes an approach, a way of looking at health, that we believe will give you better results on your healing journey. The approach we suggest is largely centered on mental and energetic perceptions and attitudes. They have worked great for us and many of our clients. However, we understand that each person is unique. Each person is responsible for making his or her own health choices. Please use your judgment about applying what you learn in this book, and draw on wisdom from other sources as well.

We urge you to make the health choices that feel best to you. Always consult a trusted health care professional about any health problems. Don't try to tackle things by yourself. We all need outside assistance. We are blessed to live at a time when there are many wonderful choices in terms of health care.

We are big proponents of using intuition when making choices. Dowsing is a method we use with good results that we feel expands our abilities to get good answers to health questions. But we never use dowsing alone to make a decision. We urge you never to make any important health decisions by using only dowsing. Be sure to get a second or even a third opinion on any major health issue. Use dowsing wisely and only as another tool in your toolkit.

CHAPTER TWO
Why Healing Is Hard

It's All About Perspective

They say that it's all about perspective. This book is about perspective. It will show you how changing your perspective can change your health.

How can a point of view be so powerful? Well, everything changes depending on the angle and distance from which you view it. To get started, we need to talk about paradigms. There are a variety of paradigms, or models, about healing and health.

Health Paradigms: Two Or More Perspectives

If you are part of Western culture, your view of health is probably based on one paradigm. That model is a collection of attitudes and beliefs that make up your perspective on health and healing. For purposes of this discussion, we'll call this paradigm the Scientific paradigm of health.

The Scientific health paradigm is just one model, but it is the dominant one in Western society. The Scientific model is based on facts or theories that are supported by scientific evidence. Unsupported beliefs may not be included. In the Scientific model, only the physical body is included in health, because only factors which can be measured may be a part of the paradigm. You may not include emotions or invisible energies that cannot be measured with an instrument.

The Scientific health paradigm is therefore quite restricted. It is not inclusive of all factors that impact your health. It only addresses factors Science has discovered and proven and measured. Since Science continues to add to its wealth of knowledge every year, it is logical to conclude that in the future, there will be far more information available for the Scientific model, and more factors that will be acceptable to the Scientific model, but for now, they are disallowed.

Because of its perspective or viewpoint, the Scientific model addresses symptoms. Symptoms are physical and measurable. The conventional health model focuses on eradicating symptoms and pain. Its biggest tools are drugs and surgery.

Since the Scientific model is the dominant paradigm for health in Western society, it is natural that insurance plays a big role. Because allopathy treats problems when they occur, you need to be able to respond when you get a symptom. And if drugs and surgery are the main treatments, you need money for them, because they are expensive. Insurance companies are supposed to help you get good health care, but they stay in business by denying claims to keep their costs down. So citizens clamor for the government to foot the bill. The government of course is using tax money to do so, which drives the cost up further.

Most people can't afford good health care anymore. At the time of writing this book, American citizens are legally required to buy into the health care program, and if they do not, they face a penalty, with few exceptions. In other words, not only is health care becoming harder to obtain at any cost; if you can't afford it or prefer another model for health, you are penalized.

When we were children, health care was affordable, but that was before Big Pharma, insurance companies and the government took over. That was a time when home remedies and over-the-counter remedies were respected more. It also seemed to be a time when there wasn't rampant cancer and heart disease and other degenerative diseases that are so common now. Health was simpler. But the perspective shifted, and now it's a mess.

There is a great deal of disillusionment with the current health care system, but very few people realize exactly why it's a problem. The problem is perspective. A growing percentage of people are defecting from the Scientific health paradigm to a holistic/alternative one. The holistic/alternative paradigm is really a reworking of the old model. In the old model, you paid for your own health care. You used natural or home remedies a lot, rather than rushing to a doctor or emergency room. You rarely used antibiotics, and you never got tests for things that weren't wrong yet. You ate healthy food and got reasonable exercise. In other words, prevention and lifestyle mattered.

In a new twist on the old time American health paradigm, the holistic/alternative paradigm addresses body/mind/spirit as a whole. It recognizes that you must look at the whole picture if you want to be healthy. Obviously, many factors cannot be measured in this model using traditional scientific instruments. So some practitioners use intuitive methods to extend their sensing abilities and gather more data.

Because in the Holistic Model you are treating the entire being on all levels, you can focus on root causes and treat them instead of symptoms. It is natural to lean towards prevention to avoid getting ill. And the remedies and methods for restoring and rebalancing health are all aimed at facilitating the body's own natural healing mechanism gently and with as few side effects as possible. This paradigm is far broader and more inclusive of all factors affecting health than the Scientific one, yet many people scoff at it.

The two health paradigms couldn't be more different. And to most people, it looks like the future of health care is about these two different paradigms slugging it out.

Some conventional professionals are hedging their bets by learning some holistic methods and then having one foot in each camp. That is integrative medicine. Integrative medicine might be regarded by some as a third paradigm, but to us it lacks a coherent viewpoint.

Now that you have seen the obvious differences in the foundation and perspective of the Scientific paradigm and the Holistic/

Alternative one, you can understand that you can't really blend the two. Integrative medicine is an attempt to cash in on the popularity of holistic methods by combining them with the insurance coverage (the biggest 'weakness' of the holistic model to many people) and the 'credibility' of the Scientific paradigm. As such, it is neither one nor the other, but it also isn't a coherent model on its own.

Getting A New Perspective
Let's go back to discussing perspective. When you have a health crisis, your main priority is to resolve your problem: get rid of the pain, get your strength back, whatever. You are looking at health close up, with your nose pressed to the window.

Change your perspective by 'backing up' a bit. Instead of only looking at getting rid of what is bothering you, step back far enough to look at your health as a whole. When you think about what health means to you, then you can choose to embrace a paradigm that makes sense to you, because it will be more likely to help you achieve your goals. In a sense, it doesn't matter which one you choose. What matters is that you make a conscious choice based on your beliefs.

It's important to realize that the different health paradigms offer completely different perspectives, and you need to choose whichever resonates with you. You will probably observe, as we have pointed out, that the allopathic method is rather restricted in scope due to its refusal to allow anything nonphysical or 'unscientific' to be considered as having impact on health. The holistic viewpoint is far broader, considering not only body, but mind/spirit as part of health. Thus, when you choose to embrace the Holistic/Alternative paradigm as a model, you are expanding your health horizons.

Beyond The Obvious Choices In Perspective
In this book, we are going to suggest you step back not only from your symptom to a larger viewpoint on health, but that you step back further and see even more of the many complex factors that impact your healing process. We will give you insights into how mind/spirit and energies affect your health, and how you can harness this knowledge to smooth and speed your own healing process. The

suggestions we make go beyond what the current Holistic/ Alternative model embraces, but we are convinced that in the near future, you will be hearing more about these subjects if you consult with a holistic doctor.

We will be outlining an approach to health that depends on your outlook and your beliefs. Change your outlook and you change your approach to health, which leads to better results. We call this 'Healing Made Simple' not because the approach we suggest is easy, but because it addresses the root cause of your health blocks and challenges. By going to the origin of your healing challenges and resolving them, you will be empowered to enjoy the health you want more easily.

The Paradox Of Perspective

What we propose is an even bigger perspective than the holistic one, with the focus being on how you can improve your healing process by focusing on yourself, your attitudes, your beliefs and actions. It would seem paradoxical to propose that by turning inward, you are expanding your viewpoint, but it is true. In order to change your perspective, you need to change how you see things, and that means changing yourself from the inside out.

We suggest that although health appears to be something most systems achieve by working on outer reality, we believe you can leverage your results and efforts by focusing more on altering your inner reality. Taking control of your health and creating the health you desire is more easily and effectively done if you focus on shifting your own energy, attitudes, beliefs and actions.

In this book, we will give you guidance on how you can take control of your healing process back by changing your perspective. By stepping back and seeing the big picture of health, you will be better able to steer yourself in the direction of your goals. You will discover some of the key ways that your viewpoint dictates or inhibits or enhances your healing process. We'll show you some positive changes you can make that will help you align with your health goals.

It's How You Look At Things

Everyone wants to feel good. But we don't notice when we feel good unless it's really special. That may be why some substances are so addictive. It is so unusual and so precious to feel really great, that we just want to do whatever it takes to get there. Sadly, that seems to lead to problems with drugs, alcohol, food and sex.

On the other hand, we all know how it feels to be sick or hurting. You weren't feeling that grateful before your symptoms appeared, but now you are disturbed with yourself for not having felt grateful. You long for the time when you weren't feeling that pain. And you'd do anything to get back to that bliss of not being in pain. But once you get back to that state, you forget to be grateful all over again.

If you are a member of Western society, you probably tend to reach for a pill to suppress the unpleasant symptom that you want to be rid of. Our culture seems to value the ability to get back to a state where we aren't feeling anything as fast as possible. Could it be that we have substituted not feeling anything for being happy, when happiness seems so hard to find?

For the first half of my life, I followed that path. When I got a pain or other symptom, I tried to find a way to erase it as much as possible. Looking back, I can see that I wasn't happy at the time, and I didn't want anyone throwing cold water on me to 'wake me up' to the life I was living. I wasn't ready or able to get the message that the path I was on was not fulfilling for me. I didn't want to face the fact that maybe I needed to make some changes.

What do you do when you get a headache or your knees give you trouble? Are you like I was, just eager to get rid of the pain and go back to a cocooned existence, wrapped in insulation? Do you judge that feeling pain is a bad thing? Do you think that no feeling at all is better than being uncomfortable and in pain?

* * *

Your perspective on health and healing drives your experience. Do you even have a viewpoint on health of which you are consciously aware? Try putting into words what your perspective is on the healing process. How do you go about being healthy? How do you regard your role in your health? Are you in charge of creating health for yourself? Or does good or bad health just 'happen'? Do you prefer to wait until something bad happens and then fix it, or do you put energy into preventing health problems? Do you treat symptoms or are you willing to take the time to discover root causes and treat them?

Most people will find that they are mute when asked to describe how they view the healing process. If they speak, they might say their health is the doctor's job, since he went to medical school for so many years to learn about it. They ask what would they know about healing and health? Or maybe they say that's why they have health insurance, so they are easily able to fix anything that goes wrong.

Long ago, I might have said the same things. I hadn't really given health much thought. I had a job with good health insurance. I had a doctor. I went to the gym to work out. I watched my weight. I tried to get good sleep. But I didn't have a coherent perspective on health and how to get or maintain it. Instead, I tended to follow the trends that were popular. For example, step aerobics was popular for exercise, so I was in a class. Years before that, running had been popular, so I ran. I didn't do these things because I had thought a lot about health. I did them because they were accepted as healthy activities, and people who wanted to be healthy did them. I followed the behavior I was told was healthy rather than thinking about health.

For good results in health, you need to have a coherent viewpoint on what you consider health to be and how you intend to go about getting and maintaining it. You are less likely to spend time on perspectives once you have a pain or symptom, so it's wise to do so beforehand, so that when faced with a problem, you already know how you want to approach resolving it.

* * *

Most people skip this important step, and that is why healing is so hard for them. They are blown like the wind with this health trend and that one, not having any structure of their own to refer to. They haven't invested in thinking about their health.

I confess I was impatient and thought-less in my younger days, wanting to just erase the symptoms and get back to living as I had been. Stepping back and looking at your viewpoint on health and healing seems a tangential way of solving health issues at best, a waste of time at worst. Yet looking back, I can see how I probably could have shaved years off my journey if I had taken this approach from the start.

I do not regret my journey. It taught me much. But in retrospect, I believe that a long, hard path is only one option. I believe that you could have a smoother, shorter path if you wish. And strangely, that path begins by not taking what you think is direct action to resolve your health problem. The short path begins by looking at your entire attitude towards and approach to health and the healing process.

Think of it this way. I can put you in a boat, plane or tractor - something you have never operated (OK, you guys who want to drive the dump truck or bulldozer, visualize that), and I can let you learn how to operate it by trial and error. If you don't kill yourself, you will figure it out eventually. And you might get the machine moving forward fairly fast. On the other hand, if you take a course in operating that machine, you will be investing a lot of time up front before you even take the wheel, but in the long run, you will be able to operate it better and more safely. Think of this book and approach as eliminating the trial and error and many potential pitfalls by investing a little time in consciously choosing how you want to approach health and healing.

Since we are each unique, I cannot promise what you will experience, but the analogy above works for me. Some people luck out when they plunge into healing looking for a fast fix. Most people ricochet from one method or healer to another, often wasting lots of time and money on few results. If you give some time and effort to the task of thinking about how you look at health and what you want to create, things will fall together faster for you, because the action you take will be in alignment with your viewpoint and goals. I wasn't blessed with that experience. I missed the signposts and got the cosmic ton of bricks dumped on me.

Years ago, in about 1990, my health finally collapsed on me. I had been a sickly child. My digestion was awful. I was allergic to dairy since birth. I had a weak immune system and suffered from many illnesses and symptoms. My parents did the best they could for me, but time and again, it looked as if they would lose me. Only when I went to college at age 18 did I make progress in creating greater health for myself. I always found that to be strange, since the diet at college was terrible, the hours were not restful and the stress incredible. Yet, I found myself feeling better than I ever had before. Suddenly, health didn't seem to be an obvious thing. Why would it be easier when I left home?

I didn't have a particular paradigm about health. I didn't think of it much, in spite of how challenging it could be for me. It wasn't until 1990 that I was forced to either give up or take control of my healing process. Thanks to the fact that I was a Biology major and stubborn about feeling good, I stepped up and began the long journey of educating myself about health; about thinking about what it meant to me; about learning all the factors that can affect health.

Some years into the journey, I was drawn into energy healing and metaphysics, and my viewpoint on healing changed forever. It was no longer enough to suppress an unwanted symptom or find a natural remedy. I wanted to resolve root causes and create the health I desired. I suddenly felt empowered to choose good health. It was liberating, and I have never looked back.

The journey was neither quick nor easy for me. It took years of study and practice to improve my health. It happened one layer at a time. I saw continual progress, but at some point, I realized that the destination of becoming healthy was not the point. It was the changes within me that took place along the way that mattered. As I changed my attitude about health, my health changed. Those changes also irrevocably changed all aspects of my life for the better.

In this book, we will share the high points of that journey with you. No two journeys are alike, but the key is to recognize that the journey is the point of it all. We will show you how to get the most out of your healing journey and to help others to do the same. It requires a change in perspective, and we will suggest ways for you to accomplish that.

You Get What You Focus On

Life isn't full of surprises. If you are conscious and aware, you find that everything makes sense and is predictable (at least after the fact). The foundation of this truth is that you get what you focus on and what you believe.

We have interacted with people who deny this angrily. They feel very downtrodden by life, and they are adamant that what has happened to them is not their fault, as if fault was a factor in health. My own mother was an excellent example of this outlook. She became terribly angry if anyone suggested she had choices in her life. My mother made many choices with regard to diet and exercise and outlook, but she never saw them as connected to her health. Instead, she acted as if things just happened to her, and she had no control over them. She felt that you were blaming her, which did not align with her picture of herself as a victim of bad situations.

Think of a bell-shaped curve (the one they used in school to determine the dreaded 'curve'). It looks like a round hill with sloping sides. This bell curve represents a group of people and their attitude on a certain subject, in this case, the creation of good health and how much control you have over it.

At one end of the curve, the part that is the base of the 'hill', there isn't much under the curve. This is a very small population of people who think they have charge of their health experience. They feel empowered to make choices, and they believe those choices will lead to better health outcomes.

In the middle, biggest part of the curve (under the hill or bell) are the majority of people. Their attitude on this subject is a sort of non-attitude. They sail along not thinking about health, or just following some trends that sound healthy. They don't think about health goals and how they might attain them other than when they occasionally go on a diet to lose a few pounds. They are pretty disconnected from

21

the process of creating good health.

On the other end of the curve (the other slope of the hill) is a small group of people who blame everything outside of themselves for their health issues. They feel totally dis-empowered, and they expect someone else to give them back their health.

I spent most of my life with the majority of people in the middle of the curve, with a slightly different attitude from my mother's, but not much greater sense of empowerment and only slightly clearer goals about what health meant to me, most of it revolving around not gaining weight and not being in pain.

What part of the curve do you inhabit? What part of the curve would you like to be in?

Though there are spectacular examples in the media, not everyone blames McDonald's for their extra weight. That is a pretty extreme position to hold, and lots of people laugh at that perspective, pointing out that no one puts a gun to your head and forces you to eat that cheeseburger. You probably don't live in that extreme portion of the curve, because those people wouldn't be interested in this book. But do you feel comfortable with the idea of taking personal responsibility for your health and for making good choices that you believe will create health for you? Or do you feel that would mean that you are to blame if you have any health issues, and you want someone else to be to blame, whether it be your doctor or your genes or our fast-food culture?

Blame is a pointless waste of time, and fearing blame tends to cause you to avoid taking responsibility You cannot create good health without taking responsibility. Once you have taken action or made a choice, you need to learn to live with it. Judging and blaming won't change the past, and it won't change the likely outcomes in your future. You need to throw those concepts in the trash for purposes of this discussion.

Personal responsibility is vital for your health. If you insist on being a victim, then you shall be a victim. What you believe is what you experience. What you focus on comes to you. What you fight, persists.

Take any of those stands at your peril. If you want to be a helpless victim of poor health, you shall receive it. How is that approach going for you? Not so good?

Pretending everything is great is equally dumb. It's vital to be honest with yourself. You need to be in touch with your emotions in order to guide your life in the path that will be best for you. If you refuse to admit you are depressed or unhappy, you will only make your health worse. Ignoring pain and symptoms won't make them go away. It makes them get 'louder'. Remember the cosmic ton of bricks? Ignoring your pain and symptoms invites the bricks to fall.

Each time you ignore a message, the next one gets 'louder'. At some point you cannot ignore the messages; whether your attention is gotten by a car accident, a heart attack or a stroke, you will have to pay attention. Don't let it go that far.

You can take control of your health to a great extent, and we are going to show you how in this book. That means you must take responsibility for your choices. Not blame. Responsibility is about the ability to respond. In other words, we are asking you to choose to respond when something happens. To be able to respond to things like symptoms in a coherent fashion.

Self-blame and guilt are also useless in the healing process. So you drank a lot of sodas and ate at McDonald's a lot for the past ten years. You can't change that. But you can make a choice to change your lifestyle if you feel it will improve your health.

Be grateful that you have the freedom to choose to a great extent what you eat and drink, whether you exercise and especially, how you think and react to things. Your health depends on these small daily choices more than you realize. Once you accept that you are responsible, you become the pilot, not the passenger, in your life.

Time and again, people have confronted me in Facebook and other forums because I am a proponent of personal responsibility. All they care about is laying blame. They don't see that when all they care about is blame, they are reinforcing powerlessness and victimhood, a vicious cycle that blocks health. They would rather be right than be healthy. This attitude is not in alignment with taking control of your health. These people give their power away. They give it to their doctors, to the health care system and to their employers or insurance providers.

If you want to blame someone for your health problems, you are telling the Universe that you are and must be a victim. Victims cannot be victors. You must give up victimhood to experience the good health you desire.

We all are victims at one time or another. Do not feel judged if you are currently feeling like a victim. Ask yourself if that is how you want to continue to feel. If not, this book is perfect for guiding you in a new path that will put you in control of your health. It can be a long journey. It might be a short one. But if you decide to be a victor, and if you do not give up, you will reach your goal.

The Challenge Of Negative Energies

In the dualistic world we live in, energies are categorized as 'negative' and 'positive' based on how we feel about them or how they make us feel. But the truest reality is that energy just is. Energy is neither good nor bad, except inasmuch as we choose to judge it.

Energies has polarity, as a magnet has a north and south pole. Like energies attract one another. But it is the opposite polarities of a given energy that attract one another most.

Here's an example: there is an energy called addiction. Let's say the positive energy expression is being addicted to a substance, while the negative expression is having a terrible repugnance to addiction. If someone has the energy of addiction, they can express it either way. This is why reformed addicts are often more zealously against addiction than non-addicts. They still have the energy of addiction and a charge on it, but the charge has flipped to the opposite expression.

It's fairly common to see an addict marry a person who hates addictions and spends a lot of time trying to reform the addict. This is because both parties have a strong charge on addiction energy, but opposite expressions of it. Addiction energy is attracted to addiction energy.

An energy that is very common in humans is victim energy. Actually, it should be called something else, because the two polar expressions of this energy are victim and victimizer. Since most people have varying degrees of victim energy (unlike addiction energy, which is less common), people have observed that everyone seems to be either one or the other, victim or victimizer. While no one would assume you have to either be an addict or hate addictions, most people assume you must be either a victim or a victimizer.

This puts you in a quandary, as neither expression is really enjoyable.

25

There is a third choice. You can be a victor. A victor does not suffer at the hands of others, because he or she lacks victim energy of either polarity. Nor does a victor hurt others who are less powerful. Whether you are expressing victim or victimizer energy, you are showing the same energy, just different polarities of it. If you want not to be a victim, you must choose to be a victor.

That sounds pretty logical when you think of it that way, doesn't it? But in reality, most people feel the either/or choice is, "I can be a victim, or I can be a victimizer." Well, that is only true if you want to express victim energy. If you decide you don't want to express victim energy, then you must choose to be a victor.

This choice requires a total change in perception. Worse yet, you can't just choose to change how you feel. You are not capable of expressing an energy you do not have. Merely being told you should be happy instead of depressed doesn't work, does it? The same is true of any energy.

Humans are drowning in victim energy. Most humans have been trained to believe that being a victimizer is bad, and that you must choose to be either a victim or a victimizer. Thus, you will see many more victims than victimizers. How many people choose to be victors? Only a small number. If you cannot see that you have a choice, you won't make it. And even if you intellectually believe you have a choice, it can be very hard to release the victim energy and embrace being a victor.

For the same reason that people are not eager to embrace personal responsibility, they are not eager to release victimhood. They believe that if they renounce victimhood, that means they are choosing to be victimizers.

If you keep the energy of a victim and renounce the expression of 'victim', you can easily become a victimizer. A good example is people who are abused as children often grow up to be abusers. They have the exact energy they had as children, but as they grow to adulthood and become capable of expressing power, they flip the polarity to victimizer. And of course, victims and victimizers attract each other.

What does all of this have to do with your health? Plenty! One reason perfect health is hard to attain is that victim energy is so common. You cannot be a powerful victim. And in order to create good health, you need to accept that you have the power to do so. You need to decide to be a victor. This is much harder than you would think. It requires a change in outlook as well as a shift in energies.

There are many modalities at this time for releasing energies and shifting them. We have used many of them. They work. What will work best for you depends on you. We suggest you research and then try one or more methods.

Tapping, The Emotion Code and The Healing Codes are just a few examples of techniques that work for many people. Before you even address any symptom and what it means, you would be wise to work on releasing victim energy and choosing to be a victor. Otherwise, all the knowledge you gain about health will do you no good. All your effort will be a waste. If you are loaded with victim energy, you will have negative experiences about health, because that is part of being a victim.

Some examples of this are:
- You may be misdiagnosed, or unable to be diagnosed
- You will have negative reactions to remedies and medications
- You will be taken advantage of by unethical health care practitioners
- You may be duped by people pretending to help you who only want your money
- You will be told you are a hypochondriac or that it's all in your head, when it isn't
- Your condition will make your life painful and a struggle
- Your health problems will impoverish you and your loved ones

* * *

Any of the above experiences could be an expression of victim energy. By removing victim energy and aligning with being a victor, you increase your chances of success many times over, before you even decide what approach to take, allopathic or holistic. Before you choose a doctor or therapy, you need to release victim energy.

Any human endeavor which is undertaken while a person has a lot of victim energy is doomed to failure. It is very hard to achieve health goals if you are loaded with the energy of powerlessness and victimhood. All of your experiences must resonate with the energy you are resonating with. This is why we say your approach to health is more important to your success than the therapy you choose.

The Lure Of Instant Fixes

Everyone wants instant gratification. It isn't just you. Human beings are inherently lazy. If they weren't, humanity would be extinct. Life in Nature is about conserving your energy for tasks that support life: gathering food, protecting yourself, finding a mate, raising your children. Any animal that puts energy into 'nonessential' tasks is likely to be removed from the gene pool, because in Nature, food isn't laid out for you. You must expend energy to find it. And you must expend energy for all important tasks. To survive you need energy, which means you must find food, and it takes energy to find food. Energy must be conserved, and that is a good working definition of 'lazy'.

So wishing you could wave a magic wand and have your pain or symptom disappear is normal. We all feel that way. The conventional health care system takes this tendency into account. In fact, it is built on the tendency to ignore health until it disappears, then to demand a quick fix to erase the symptoms with as little investment of energy as possible. We can fuss all we want about the grim state of the sick care system, but it grew up and became strong in response to what the majority of people are demanding. They want someone to fix them after they are broken; they want a fast fix; they don't want to pay for it or to have any responsibility in their healing process.

How's that working for you? As long as I had a modicum of health, I was fine with it. I wasn't sick more than once or twice a year. I'd get the flu once a year like clockwork (until I stopped taking the flu shots). I'd get a cold a couple times a year. But really, that didn't seem so bad compared to my childhood. I could take over-the-counter remedies and get through it ok. It was only when my health became critically endangered that the system stopped working for me. It was terrifying to see my health and energy levels deteriorate no matter what I did, and the doctors seemed mystified as to what was wrong. To a great extent, they said nothing was really wrong, because they could not figure it out.

* * *

Perhaps you've been in the situation where the doctor says you are imagining your problem. My mother had an accident when my youngest sister was a baby. Mom would take Terry out in her baby carriage on sunny days. It was a huge, heavy and old-fashioned one, not the kind you can get today that folds down and is lightweight. One day, Mom was manhandling it down the steep hill in front of our house to get to the sidewalk, but the grass was wet and she slipped. Not wanting to let go of the carriage, she took the fall badly, hurting her back.

She was in great pain and went to the emergency room and had X-rays taken. The doctors pronounced that there was nothing wrong with her in spite of her saying the pain was awful. For years, she struggled with back pain, but didn't say much about it, because the doctors had said it was all in her head. Many years after the accident, she got an X-ray for an unrelated problem. The doctor was reading the X-rays and said conversationally, "So when did you break your back?"

As a former Level III radiographer at NASA, I now know that X-rays are notoriously hard to read and don't always tell the whole story, especially when you are looking for cracks. So why did the doctors not listen to her? They must have been aware of this fact. Time and again I have seen this attitude of 'it's all in your mind' if the test results don't show anything.

Yet the doctors meant no harm. Their approach is so focused on looking at test results and numbers that they often ignore the big picture, the whole body. Also, because in the current system, people give their power to doctors, it is expected that the doctors know all and the patient should never contradict the doctor. We expect a doctor to tell us what is going on and what to do, and doctors aren't comfortable saying, "I don't know."

I'm not going to complain about the system. The weaknesses of the system have propelled me and many other people onto a much-needed healing journey. We got awakened to the deficiencies in how we were approaching health, and we started to look at things in new ways. It was a rude awakening for most of us. It can be painful and embarrassing to challenge the old way of looking at health. Often, it is hard to get support when you decide the system isn't working for you.

We all want instant fixes. When the system can't deliver them, that can be a sign that you are ready to start thinking of health in new and more constructive ways. Instant fixes are usually about covering up symptoms, not about resolving causes. As the health care system becomes more overburdened, it seeks ways to limit expenses, and treating symptoms becomes more and more the norm, because that is cheaper and faster than looking for causes and treating them.

Maybe you have picked up this book simply because you intuitively know that healing is a journey and takes time and effort and probably a change of attitude. More likely, you are like me and many others who have always wanted instant fixes, and when the system couldn't provide any fix at all, much less a quick one, it was like a bucket of ice water waking you up to a new reality.

Now you are ready to see things in new ways, because you know there must be a way to get the health you want. That's good, because your commitment to seeing things in new ways is going to propel you down a path that will change your life forever. You will find yourself learning to value patience and seeing the opportunities in each situation instead of pointlessly trying to control outcomes over which you have no real control.

Healing Is A Journey

You have probably heard that healing takes place in layers, and that healing is a journey. These are valid descriptions, and we hear a lot of people saying them, but in reality, most people want instant fixes. As we said in the previous section, when the cosmic ton of bricks lands on you and destroys your health, that often puts you on a different path in life, because the instant fixes you desire are no longer an option. You have to start looking at health in new ways. That is when we start hearing people talk about healing being a journey and healing in layers, like peeling an onion.

As much as you hear these expressions among metaphysical people, it isn't common to find someone who is actually enjoying the journey to perfect health. When you feel unhealthy, you are cranky and understandably impatient to return to a healthy condition. You aren't the least bit interested in taking a journey to health. To heck with peeling layers off. You want to feel good now.

When one doctor, remedy or modality doesn't give you what you want, you move on to the next, and the next and the next. While it is important to persevere if you wish to reach your goals, you will go through a lot of trials and spend a lot of time and money if all you are focused on is the destination of feeling good.

We've worked with clients for years, and it is very common to be drawn into that vicious cycle of seeking health, of chasing after it. If you are only fixated on getting rid of what ails you and feeling good, then you are ignoring the message your body is sending you. You obsess with how nothing is changing. You focus on what's wrong instead of what you want. As the Law of Attraction teaches us, this will lock dis-ease in place.

Pain and symptoms are like telegrams from your High Self, your Inner Self or the part of you that sees the bigger picture, telling you what energy you are resonating with. The symptoms can be regarded as specific messages that you can take action on and change your life by changing your energy and outlook, or they can be regarded as a pain in the neck that you just want to get rid of, so you can get back to living the same way you always have.

The latter attitude is the most common, and it's the reason so many people are not that healthy. What happens if you keep getting telegrams from your mortgage company that your payments are in arrears and you just throw them out, because they cause you pain and embarrassment? Keep acting that way to suppress your pain, and you will end up losing your house. On the other hand, you can face the painful facts and try to find a resolution to the problem of being in arrears on your mortgage. Solving the root cause will allow you to remove both the pain and the fear of losing your home.

It's quicker and easier to tear up the notices and ignore them. It's much harder to face your financial problem and try to find a solution so you can live happily in your house. But the latter is obviously the way to go. So it's a balance between facing what is and moving forward to create what you want.

Now, continuing the same analogy, you are behind in your mortgage payments because of some energy or behavior. Maybe you are spending more than you are earning. Maybe you lost your job and have no income. Whether your problem is overspending or job loss, it will take time and effort to face and change things so that you don't have those problems anymore. You can't wave a magic wand over problems like that.

Thus, it will be a journey to achieve your goal of catching up on your mortgage payments. Perhaps if you accept the journey and start down the road, you might end up leaving your house for a less expensive one to restore your security.

Change is inevitable. The only question is will you suppress the message because you don't want the pain, or will you accept the journey and spend the time to discover what needs to change so that you can be happy?

* * *

Healing of all kinds is like that. The pain and symptoms in your body or in your finances or relationships are messages. There are many wonderful resources for deciphering the messages from your body. See the Resources for books we use. But those reference guides won't attract you, nor will those methods resonate with you unless you adopt a new approach to healing.

The healing journey takes time, but most of all, it requires you to change. You need to change your outlook, your beliefs, your reactions and/or your behavior. Your current viewpoint and choices and subconscious beliefs have had a big role in your current situation. Other factors you aren't aware of like karmic ones and family patterns, things you can't see a way of controlling, also contribute to your health.

Along the journey to good health, you will be challenged to see things in new ways. Maybe you don't believe in past lives or karma. But it does explain a lot of health issues. Perhaps you have no knowledge of subconscious beliefs, but they do affect your ability to heal and how much trouble it is. Your health is about way more than just your dietary choices, although those are very important.

If you start on a healing journey with an open mind, you probably won't recognize yourself when you reach your destination. The reason for that is, you cannot be the same exact person you are now and have totally different health from what you are now experiencing. Change is required.

If you are determined to restore your health without changing yourself, you will fight a losing battle. And if you are angry about the things you must shed along the path, the journey will be a struggle.

For a great part of my healing journey, I was very 'serious'. I tended to focus on the health I didn't have and the symptoms I didn't like. It took a lot of time, effort and money for me to heal, in part because of my focus and the beliefs I had.

There are people who say healing is easy. Just wave a crystal or say a prayer or spin a pendulum with intention.

Healing can be simple, but it usually is not easy. Good health is a precious possession, and we tend to believe that valuable things cost a lot of money to maintain and once lost, are difficult to get back. It isn't surprising that most people experience this version of reality which makes healing a struggle.

What if you truly believed on all levels of your being that healing is simple and easy? Then you would find it to be a more pleasant journey.

In this book, we will show you a number of ways that you can change your outlook and approach to healing to make it more simple and easier. Don't expect everything to click into place overnight. You need time to shift those energies. Allow yourself to enjoy the process of accepting that healing can be simple; that your body has a miraculous intelligence that allows it to heal with very little outside help in many cases; that the journey to health can be an awakening and enlightening experience.

Self-test

After reading this chapter, you perhaps are aware that the biggest challenges you face are in changing how you perceive health and the healing process. Growing up in the culture I did, I looked outward for healing. Advances in medicine and surgery and testing methods was our measure of progress in terms of being able to create good health.

The facts have not stood up to the expectations we all had. Cancer and heart disease are as much or more of a threat than ever. Good health is amazingly elusive in the richest countries on earth. Why would that be? Logically, one would assume that the higher the technology and the more healing methods available, the better the overall health of a population would be.

Although infant death and malnutrition and some other acute problems that shortened life spans historically are not a problem in modern cultures, the overall health of the population is not that great. We may live longer average lives than our forbears, but we find our health deteriorating at an age when we should still be enjoying life. Obesity is epidemic. And degenerative diseases are robbing older folks of happy golden years. Depression and other psychological ailments seem far more common than in the past.

Is this a necessary evil of extending the life expectancy in modern societies, or is it some fundamental energetic expression of a perception that good health is hard to keep or we must decline with age? Historically, fewer people survived to live to old age, and those who did were fairly vigorous. Now, more people live to past 70, but not without reams of health issues, prescription drugs and ailments that limit their ability to live a meaningful, comfortable existence.

What if these observed patterns were due to outlook rather than genes? Take the following self-test and see how much you are in alignment with good health and with being empowered to create it.

* * *

Answer the following questions 'yes' or 'no'. Choose the answer that is closest to what you think is true on the average. Don't answer what you think is expected of you or is the 'best' answer. Be honest and say how you feel inside.

1. Overall do you believe that you have significant control over whether you experience good health or not?

2. Do you spend significant time thinking about what good health means to you and how you would define and measure it? In other words, can you give a clear explanation of how you would know you were in good health that involves NO negative statements such as "no pain'?

3. Have you mastered and do you use a healing modality/remedies of any kind (herbs, oils, EFT, The Emotion Code) on a regular basis?

4. Do you have a process by which you consider carefully whether or not you really need to consult a doctor when symptoms appear for you or a pet or family member? (As opposed to running off to the doctor or ER or vet right away)

5. Have you worked on finding an exercise regimen that helps you stay fit and healthy, and that you practice regularly, even only 2 or 3 times a week?

6. Do you have a diet you have consciously chosen as a healthy way of eating to support your body nutritionally, whether it is gluten-free, paleo or vegetarian? (As opposed to following a trend or just eating whatever you feel like, maybe feeling a bit guilty about your choices.)

7. Are you willing to make choices that seem odd and even freaky to your family or friends if you believe it will help keep you healthy? (As in, you aren't afraid to use holistic methods and energy healing even if they think it's crazy).

8. Do you do regular detoxes of any kind for your physical body? (This can involve fasting, taking trace minerals, colonics and other similar methods)

9. Do you do regular space clearing of your living space and/or work space? (Waving a sage wand around isn't adequate, but for the purposes of this test, say 'yes' if you do even that much clearing regularly, as in at least every few months.)

10. Do you believe in invisible factors that can affect your health, and

have you studied or learned how to resolve them, and do you put those practices in place? (As in clearing entities, checking for curses and noxious environmental energies and things like astrological factors and boundary issues.)

There are no right or wrong answers to this test. It merely gives you a chance to see what your approach to health and healing is. We will be making a case in this book for taking control of your health back, and so we are giving 1 point to each 'yes' answer.

Tally the number of 'yes' and 'no' answers you have. The more 'yes' answers you have, the more empowered your viewpoint on health. 8 to 10 'yes' answers is a sign of a winning attitude. 5-7 is way above average. 0-4 means you will benefit from adjusting your attitude even more if you wish to take control of your health.

CHAPTER THREE
What Is Health To You?

Get Clear What Health Is

You probably can't give a quick, clear answer to the question, "What is good health to you?" If you can, congratulations, it's obvious you've thought a lot about this subject. Focusing on what good health means to you is an important step in taking charge of your healing process. After all, you need to know where you're headed on this journey.

If you cannot answer the question easily or if your answer is a bunch of things you don't want to experience, such as, "Good health is not having headaches all the time," then we've started at a good place for you. It's vital that you have a clear picture of what good health is before you set out to try and create it. And knowing what you don't want is a first step in the process.

Knowing what you mean by good health will change how you look at healing, and without this, you aren't going to be able to change your approach to health and get better results.

You aren't alone if you haven't given much thought to the question of what good health means to you. Most of us don't really spend much time thinking about what good health is until we lose it. Then we tend to think of it as getting rid of the pain we are suffering with, no more than that. It is that lack of clarity and focus about health that is the weak foundation we have built our healing approaches on, and we need to rebuild a good foundation. It is also that focus on getting rid of symptoms that has led to the current paradigm on health that focuses only on symptoms.

You would think that as we age, we have so many experiences of good and bad health that we would find it easy to describe what good health is. Instead, it seems that most mature adults just accept that decrepitude and pain is part of the aging process, and they go on focusing on what's wrong with their health with little hope of restoring strength and vigor.

There are many ways you can approach this question about what health is to you. One easy way is to make a list of all the things that are wrong with your health. You might include things like insomnia, low energy, allergies, indigestion and headaches.

Once you've thought about what's wrong with your health, what's stopping you from feeling healthy, then you can think of what the opposite is. The opposite is what you want to experience. So you might say you want to experience having a deep, restful sleep each night; having plenty of energy to do whatever you feel like; being able to eat anything you like with good digestion and feeling comfortable in your body all the time.

You will probably find that it takes you a while to think what the opposite of each of your symptoms is. That is because you've spent so much time thinking about what's wrong, what is, that you haven't focused on what you want to create. The Law of Attraction makes it quite clear that if you want to create something, you must not focus on the lack of it or what is. You must focus on what it is you wish to experience. What you focus on is what you are creating.

Your initial reaction to doing this exercise and having to focus on what you want instead of what is will probably spark some resistance and irritation in you. You will feel like justifying your current pattern. There are two reasons not to do that. The first is rather obvious. If this pattern hasn't given you what you want, it makes sense to change it. Justification just cements a negative pattern in place. And secondly, the resistance and irritation are just a sign you fear making changes. They are actually telling you that this is a good direction for you to go in, even though it is outside your comfort zone.

After all, if your comfort zone is being ill, having nasty symptoms and not having the health you desire, you don't want to stay in it, do you? So let's get started changing that pattern.

Set Goals For Health

You've thought about what good health means to you. It's important that you be detailed and specific in defining it. Because the next step in changing your attitude and approach to health involves setting health goals.

Setting goals is a pretty standard procedure when you want to make changes. You need goals to direct your progress and to allow you to measure it.

You've given some thought to what you would call good health. What kinds of goals can you create that go along with your definition? Here are some examples:

If you have really low energy, but you think having good health would mean having enough energy to go out dancing every Saturday and enjoy it, then that becomes a goal. Going out dancing and enjoying it and having plenty of energy is measurable and a good way to see progress.

Perhaps you have seasonal allergies that make you miserable each spring during pollen season. Your idea of good health might be that you could enjoy the entire spring season feeling able to breathe easily and having clear eyes that feel good. This is a goal that is measurable.

Perhaps your digestion is so bad that you only have a few things you can eat that don't upset you. You might think that good health would be eating anything you wish and feeling comfortable afterwards. A reasonable goal might be to be able to enjoy eating one particular type of food that's been giving you problems, something you consider a treat, with no side effects.

Goals should be attainable, or you can become discouraged. Always pick goals that seem reasonable. But they should also be something you really would like to experience.

* * *

You might be wondering how you can set goals if you have a degenerative disease or a genetic condition that has no cure. What can you set as reasonable goals then? That is going to depend totally on you. There are health conditions that are very difficult to change, and indeed, some that probably aren't going to change no matter what you do.

You cannot know why you attracted this health problem. Maybe it is just a message from your body to make some changes. Perhaps it is just to 'wake you up'. On the other hand, sometimes we come into this life and choose to experience a very unpleasant physical situation for other reasons, such as for personal growth or maybe even to help others. Christopher Reeves comes to mind. His condition was not 'fixable'. Yet he used it to spread hope and lift the spirits of people who had handicaps like his. There is no telling how many people he helped with his courage and grace. Sometimes, your goal may be simply to have courage and grace in the face of a seemingly impossible health problem.

Only you can decide what a reasonable goal is for your health. Once you decide on it, you must commit to it. Having a goal is worthless if you lack commitment. You can have the goal of being fit, but if you do not commit to it, nothing will change.

Commitment won't get you much if you don't have a plan for achieving your goal. Whatever goal you set, you then need to have concrete steps you can follow which you believe will help bring you closer to success. Believing in the ability to succeed is a key part of success, and your action plan helps you have that level of belief as well as giving you rituals that anchor your intention during the process.

Your action plan will be tailored to your goals, your budget and what you believe. If you want to get fit, you may start exercising regularly, or quit smoking, or give up junk food. Or a combination of things.

Sometimes it's really obvious what you need to do. You've just been putting it off because you didn't feel like doing it. Other times you have no clue what to do. What do you do in situations like that? If you have a goal that you feel you can achieve, but you just aren't sure what to do, then you probably need to do some research and consult with some experts who can guide you.

For example, if you have allergies or digestive issues, you may feel you don't understand the human body well enough to know how to go about reaching your health goals. Maybe if you have Biology degrees like I did, you can read the many books and check out all the websites on the internet that address your issue. But even I didn't try to go it completely alone. I found experts to guide me: chiropractors, naturopaths, homeopaths. I took courses in healing methods. I studied herbs and supplements and flower essences and essential oils.

How much you do on your own will depend on your confidence and experience in the subject you are addressing. Don't be afraid to get outside assistance to help you put a reasonable plan together for reaching your health goals. There are plenty of helpers out there.

One thing to remember as you work through this process of setting goals, making a plan and committing to action is that it is best to be flexible. I don't mean flexible in terms of following your plan or not. I mean flexible in terms of tweaking it as needed along the way.

If you see health as a journey, you can consider your goals and plan like a roadmap. The roadmap seems to say a certain path is the swiftest and easiest way to your destination. But when you get on the actual road, you sometimes come upon road works or a big traffic tie-up or a major accident. Or maybe the weather along that path is so bad it makes travel slow and treacherous. If you aren't willing and able to adapt as you follow your path, you will find yourself struggling more often than you would like.

Be willing to pause and re-evaluate your route and make changes based on recent experience and the knowledge you have gained from it. Perhaps you will switch from yoga to running for exercise, or you might go from chiropractic to naturopathy. You didn't plan that when you set out, but based on results, you feel it's time to make some changes. And you feel ok doing that. Being open to changing what you do will help you have a smoother, easier journey.

Lastly, you need to be able to measure progress. We all need reinforcement when we are making an effort to create new habits. You are working to manifest a new way of being. You want to be healthier. It supposedly takes about 4 weeks of constant effort to create a new habit, so it behooves you to measure your progress and confirm that what you are doing is bringing you closer to your goals.

Celebrate milestones. If you are trying to get fit, you may celebrate losing a certain amount of weight or being able to bench press a certain weight. You may celebrate finishing your first 10K race, or your first spring without having to take Benadryl constantly. Joy and gratitude help reinforce a behavior and they also attract more to be joyful and grateful for. So try and find ways to measure progress and then celebrate them.

Goals Exercise

The material in this chapter is so important, that it is worth doing an exercise to get your goals clearly stated and have an action plan, along with milestones for measuring progress. Take the time to answer these questions. Date the work and put it aside. Mark your calendar to go back in six months and see about your progress. Good luck!

Step 1

Make a very specific and detailed list of what good health means to you. NOT what you won't be experiencing, but what you will be experiencing when you have good health.

Things to consider are energy level, activities you would like to participate in, things you would be able to do that you cannot easily do now and other physically measurable achievements.

You will also want to include emotions, like feeling more comfortable in your body, happier with your life and other positive emotions that you may not be experiencing as much as you would like at this time.

Step 2

Create an action plan that you believe will help you reach your goals. It may be a dietary or exercise regimen or regular work with a particular method like chiropractic or Reiki. Be specific and list the actions you believe you need to take in order to reach your goals.

Be sure to include things YOU do. It's fine to include seeing a professional for massage or other treatments, but it is vital to see yourself as the main person responsible for your health. You might want to plan on committing to using Louise Hay's book "You Can Heal Your Life" to look up the energetic and emotional causes of physical symptoms so you can then tap on them or do The Emotion Code or shift energy using whatever method you like.

* * *

You can commit to a practice of gratitude daily, or of meditation or of journaling to list all the positive things that happened that day. There are many actions you can take to help yourself become more centered, feel more empowered and focus on the positive. Create a good mix of your own efforts plus outside help from professionals for best results.

Remember to have alternate plans and be open to changing course as needed along the way, depending on results.

Step 3
Set some milestones so you can measure and celebrate progress. Don't just have one big goal that is far off. Have several small events that will allow you to celebrate change. If you want to be fit and feel you need to lose 20 pounds, celebrate each time you lose 5 pounds. If you want to run a marathon but never trained to run, celebrate the first time you run a mile, then a 10K race.

Step 4
It's always helpful to find a group to journey with. The group should be focused on the positive and not sit around complaining. They should be like-minded to you. Look for people who will support you when you are feeling a bit down and who will help you re-focus and stay committed to your path.

Step 5
Identify professionals and experts and resources so that you aren't totally on your own in your journey. Maybe you just use a lot of information from the internet. Or you have a Reiki practitioner you see regularly. No one can make huge changes all by themselves. While you are the most important person in this project, it is much easier to get results if you aren't totally alone on your journey.

CHAPTER FOUR
The Energy Body vs. The Physical Body

Everything Starts In The Energy Body

In this chapter, we may be preaching to the choir, but it's important to mention this subject, as it was one of the first major ahawo (the actual plural of 'aha') that I had on my healing journey that triggered a new approach. So it's important we make sure you are on board with this before we go much further.

You are more than your physical body, and your health consists of much more than your physical body appearing to be healthy. There are invisible aspects to your being that contribute greatly to the state of your health. Your subtle energy body, which is the subject of many excellent books and courses, has energetic layers. The condition of those layers contributes to your health. Or detracts from it.

Those who recognize the energy body as part of the whole human usually believe that good health or bad health starts in the energy body. If you have damage to your energy body on any layer and it is not treated and the insult persists, you will eventually end up with a physical symptom. Consider the energy damage like a physical symptom, but you don't notice it as easily. If you ignore or try to suppress symptoms, you are not restoring your body's balance. If you ignore or fail to treat energy problems, they will lead to health issues later.

In this book we use a lot of examples that involve your physical symptoms. It's important to understand that the root causes of those symptoms, which we discuss in the next chapter, almost always begin in your energy body.

* * *

Being aware of this should lead you to be interested in making the health of your energy body a priority. The stronger and healthier your energy body, the healthier your physical body will be. It pays to take care of your energy body. In a later chapter, we will introduce you to an intuitive technique that will make this much easier to do.

Regular care and maintenance of your energy body with the intention of repairing damage, restoring balance and strengthening it will improve your results in all your health goals. This is a vital shift in your approach to health. Not only are you going to become more proactive and look at symptoms differently; you will start putting more and more focus on making your energy body healthy, as that is where good health begins.

There are many things you can do to help with this. Energy healing modalities are wonderful. Meditation is helpful. Keeping your space clear is important. Regular energy clearing is terrific. Working on shifting worn out patterns and beliefs is useful. Releasing negative emotions helps.

It's obvious that there is no one method that will address all of these things. So making the commitment to add tools to your toolkit that address these issues is a good goal. Don't be concerned or overwhelmed. It took us literally years to put together a good toolkit, but it has paid off. You will see ongoing progress if you take this approach. It is a vital aspect of making healing simpler.

Don't Neglect The Physical Body

While in the last section, we emphasized the value of tending to the subtle energy body, we have observed that people often choose either the physical or energetic body to focus on, rather than caring for both in equal measure.

The tendency to focus on the energy body, hoping that treatment of the physical body won't be needed, sometimes is a symptom of a subconscious or conscious discomfort with the physical realm. Many unhealthy people are unhealthy in part because of the belief that earth is a dangerous and unpleasant place. Others have a disgust of the physical body at some level. The negative feelings and beliefs lead to the manifestation of negative physical experiences.

You may or may not be aware of how deeply you are affected by these influences. If you attempt to put new practices in place, caring for your physical body, but you meet with challenges, you may need to deal with subconscious issues about the body or the physical plane of existence. It is beyond the scope of this book to go into details on various techniques, but there are many which claim to deal with subconscious blocks. You can research our websites, courses and services for our take on this important subject.

It is unlikely that you will ever experience the health you desire if you persist in believing the earth is a terrible place where everyone must suffer. Once again, you can see how a change in perspective is vital in order for you to have different results from the ones you've been having.

Conventional people tend to do the opposite and focus only on the physical body. That is sort of like closing the barn door after the horse has gotten out. If all you ever pay attention to is your physical body, you will probably have to invest a lot of time in your health. When you fix one thing, another will break down. Stepping back and looking at the big picture of health will help you overcome this problem.

The optimal perspective is to tend to both your subtle energy body and physical body. Using whatever methods are appropriate to balance and heal on all levels will give you better results overall. Don't just do Reiki or tapping. Evaluate your diet and use supplements as needed. Investing in caring for both the energetic and physical is a new perspective for most people, but you will see better results if you adopt this approach.

CHAPTER FIVE
Root Causes vs. Symptoms

What Are Root Causes?

Part of your new approach to healing will involve focusing on root causes as opposed to symptoms. Our current health care system focuses mainly on getting rid of symptoms, and sometimes it is quite effective at that. Take a pill, and your headache disappears. Your fever drops into a safe zone. Your cough goes away. It's almost like a miracle.

But what if those symptoms have a purpose? By causing you to be uncomfortable, they get your attention. That is a good thing, because if you react to them appropriately, you can then find out what the message is that your body is sending you. Symptoms are the only way your body can let you know your health is out of balance. So, suppressing symptoms is like burning your first class mail rather than reading it.

Your body has an amazing self-healing process, but it can get out of balance. It can get blocked. As you get older, the poor lifestyle choices you got away with as a younger person begin to pile up. Sooner or later the bill comes due, and your body sends you a message in the form of a symptom, saying, "Hey, there's a problem you need to address." It has to do it that way, because otherwise you'd never know you were out of balance.

The great part is, if you learn to read the messages, you can take appropriate action and resolve the imbalance and return to health. As we mentioned earlier, most people suppress symptoms and basically ignore the messages. So the messages have to get 'louder'. If you keep ignoring them, at some point you get hit by the 'ton of bricks' and have a major health collapse. This happens because you didn't pay attention to the earlier, quieter messages. Just think how much trouble you could save if you changed your approach and started reading those messages and acting appropriately to resolve your health imbalances.

A 'root cause' is the original imbalance or problem. The symptom you experience is the message your body gives you to tip you off to what the root cause is. Depending on whom you speak with, a root cause might be defined as either physical or energetic. People who take a more conventional viewpoint will be content to find a physical root cause of a symptom. So they might find that the migraines they are experiencing are caused by eating chocolate. (Oh dear!)

If you have that viewpoint, taking the time to discover that chocolate triggers your migraines is wonderful, because then you don't have to take expensive prescription drugs with nasty side effects to get rid of the migraines. You won't have them as long as you avoid chocolate. Although we live in a society that seems to accept being drugged to the eyeballs, almost anyone would agree it's better not to have to take drugs if you can avoid it. (Well, at least everyone except the makers of drugs…)

But can you take it back even further, tracing root causes beyond the physical into the invisible realm of energies and emotions and beliefs? Yes, you can. Doing so takes you into the realm of healing as personal growth. Those who have this outlook believe that in order to restore balance and health, you often need to release or transform energies: beliefs, emotions and trauma from this life or others. When you accomplish that, you have cleared the root cause of your health issue, and good health can be more easily restored.

In other words, not only can you not be healed just by suppressing a symptom. You can't truly restore balance if all you look at is the physical body. The reason for that is that all health problems start in your energy body. In order to create harmony and balance in your physical body, you need to discover the energetic root cause of the problem and deal with it.

This is a much more challenging goal. In fact, it would seem impossible except for the pioneers who have provided us with wonderful 'dictionaries' of the energetic causes behind physical symptoms and conditions. There are links to our favorite reference guides in the Chapter Thirteen - Resources section. Think of these guides as your dictionaries for translating foreign phrases when you are on a trip. They really are that easy to use, taking the biggest challenge you face in this process and making it simple.

Investing in these guides empowers you to take charge of your healing process. While you will still need outside help on occasion, you will be approaching health in a totally new way. You are saying that you intend to do your best to restore your health whenever you can by treating energetic root causes.

Taking this step probably isn't so challenging if you've been a spiritual seeker or studied energy medicine. But it is a huge step nonetheless. Whether you realize it or not, this change in approach puts you into a whole different paradigm of health. You will be in a minority, but don't worry. You'll start seeing results and soon wish to persuade others to see things your way. (Don't spend a lot of time on that. It usually doesn't work.)

If treating symptoms doesn't work, why does everyone do it? They do it because getting out of pain is a priority for most people. Once they get rid of their pain, they can go back to living their lives just as they were before. Getting rid of the pain is their definition of success.

But when you see the symptom as a message about an imbalance you need to address, it's obvious that getting rid of the symptom is the last thing you want to do. You want to decipher the message your body is sending, then fix the problem, because then the symptom can go away on its own.

This outlook is so revolutionary that most people can't get their heads around it. Almost everyone who has this viewpoint has come to it through their own pain and suffering. Many had the ton of bricks land on them and rob them of their health. And the only way back was to take a new approach, which they did. But trying to convince others who aren't desperate to restore their lost health that taking a pill is a waste of time and counterproductive is a hard thing to sell. Taking a pill is so easy. And the pain goes away. What else matters? These people define health differently from us. They think the absence of pain is good health. You know better now.

Treating Root Causes Is A Challenge

It sounds exciting to treat root causes instead of suppressing symptoms, but there is another reason that this paradigm hasn't caught on. It's much harder to discover and resolve root causes than it is to suppress a symptom. Implied in this outlook is that you are taking a more active role in creating good health for yourself. That is certainly a good idea, but if you've spent your life going to a doctor whenever you have a bad symptom and letting the doctor write you a prescription, you may feel a bit lost at this point.

What we've said so far makes a lot of sense, but when you start to apply it, you run into difficulties. Even if you buy the reference guides we mentioned earlier, how can you be sure which explanation is YOUR root cause? There are often multiples possible causes listed for any symptom.

Then, if you figure out which root cause is your problem, what do you do to fix it? Maybe you are fortunate enough to have learned a healing technique such as Reiki or The Emotion Code. But you are aware that there are no one-size-fits-all solutions. How can you decide what to do? And even if you can, how do you apply it?

We've only just started to build a foundation for the new approach to healing. There are some key elements we're going to address in the next few chapters. These are all part of creating a solid approach that anyone can follow and get results. You are totally transforming the way you look at health; how you measure health and how you react to an apparent imbalance in your health. If you've been following holistic health trends in recent years or you practice alternative methods, you will find yourself in agreement with many of the statements made thus far. But are you really practicing what you believe, or have you merely added it onto a conventional approach to health?

The next few chapters are the most challenging, because they weave together key ideas and offer valuable tools for practicing a new approach to healing. Taken individually, some or even all of these elements may seem familiar, but you probably haven't seen them set out as a coherent way of thinking about health and taking control of your healing process.

There is no doubt that part of the reason this paradigm hasn't taken off is because it requires more effort on your part than going to a doctor does. Don't let that prospect overwhelm you. Remember, healing is a journey. And as you travel your healing path, you will have a chance to learn many new things. Your perceptions will change. It won't happen overnight. Before we embark on the next step, do the simple exercise in the next section. It demonstrates how you will approach symptoms with this newfound paradigm.

Exercise
A Step-By-Step Approach To Finding Root Causes

- Think of a symptom you have had recently, or one that you have often. An example might be pain in your right knee; gastritis; insomnia.

- Go to your Reference guide. Having more than one guide is quite useful. We love "Messages From The Body", but it is rather expensive. If you are new to this, start with Louise Hay's "You Can Heal Your Life". It will be a great starting point. Then, if you find you love doing this, get Michael Lincoln's book. It's absolutely amazing. Look up your physical symptom in the reference guide. Sometimes you can gather additional information by looking at more general terms as well, such as 'pain'. Go from the more specific symptom to the more general terms.

- If you cannot find anything that matches your symptom, you need a better reference guide. You can go online and see if you can find anything by Googling the symptom and looking for the energetic meaning of it.

- In most cases you will find more than one meaning listed. Look at each one and with brutal honesty, tune in and see which one or ones most resonate with you.

- The purpose of this is to find the energy behind your symptom, the message from your body. If you don't want to hear the message, you won't be able to heal. Many newbies will find they resist admitting to having any energy they judge as 'negative'. This is normal. Just push through it. You will find this approach will strip you of ego and help you become more authentic. That alone is priceless.

- Once you settle on what the message is, think carefully about how it relates to you as an individual. Can you think of examples in your life and your relationships that form a pattern of this energy? For example, if the energy is one of self-judgment and shame, where do you think it could have originated? Were you brought up in a fundamentalist religion that preached hellfire and damnation? Did you have critical parents? Was your schooling unpleasant and demeaning?

- Think about individual instances where you remember these energies being strong. Do you still have a charge on those incidents? Do you feel bad when you think about them? This is a sign that you need to do some work to transform and release those energies so you can heal.

- Pick a method that you believe can accomplish this transformation. It may be a method you do, such as tapping. Or you may need to consult with a counselor. When the session is done, revisit the incidents and note your level of emotion. If you were successful, you will feel much closer to neutral about the events.

- Releasing the past; forgiveness; taking responsibility without blaming; feeling empowered; establishing harmony and peace. These are the goals of working with the root causes. These are the changes that will allow healing to take place.

- Repeat this process whenever you get a symptom, especially any pattern of symptoms that repeat.

- Seek outside help if you don't see a noticeable change.

CHAPTER SIX
Make Intuition Part Of Your Healing Process

Expand Your Intelligence

You make health choices all the time. Most of them you do almost by rote. It's pretty easy to know when you need to go to the Emergency Room. When you have a broken bone or a life-threatening infection, it's foolish to mess about with it on your own. At the opposite end of the spectrum are the simple problems that crop up now and then. A cold, a 48-hour virus, a skin rash. You have over-the-counter remedies and enough experience to resolve them yourself with confidence. You always know that if things get worse, you can go to the doctor.

But what about the gray zone, that area in between the obvious extremes of the ER and doing it yourself? Depending on your personality, confidence, experience and training, that gray zone will be either rather large or somewhat narrow. But it's always there.

When a situation comes up that falls in the gray zone, you don't automatically know what to do. You still have the same goals as ever, but you aren't sure of the best way to attain them. You are suddenly aware of the cost of a mistake. If you fail to go to the vet or doctor for a serious condition, your pet could die, or your life could be at risk. On the other hand, going to the vet or doctor could be an unnecessary waste of time, money and effort.

We've all been there. And what we choose to do is guess. Because we have no other option. We will guess with whatever our personal prejudice is. Some will err on the side of caution and invest money and time in the doctor or vet regardless of how necessary. Others will look at their budget and hold off investing, because they just don't feel they have the money. Guessing is bad enough and likely to lead to mistakes, but guessing based on money, fear or judgment compounds the problem.

We've all done it: misjudged a health situation, either for good or ill. Wouldn't it be great not to have to guess? Health is so important, we really need to get rid of that gray zone or at least minimize it.

Well, we have a suggestion for how you can do that. Your rational mind can't get the right answers in a situation like that, but your intuitive sensing can. However, it needs to be properly trained and practiced to use the skill well.

Your body has a natural knowing ability, and your heart speaks the language of intuition fluently. If you call on this ability, you can narrow the gray zone down to almost nothing.

Before I even tell you how to do that, I can hear you asking, "What if I make a mistake, though?" Well, guesswork is never better than 50/50, and if you hone this skill, you can improve on those odds quite a bit. It isn't perfect. Nothing in life is 100% foolproof. But with practice, it can be over 90% accurate. And that will really save you a lot. So are you ready to hear about this amazing technique?

Get Answers

Your intuition is the other type of intelligence you have. Your rational mind is good at gathering data and analyzing it. But if there isn't enough data and nothing to analyze, it can't function. We've all been there, having to make a decision without enough data. And since there's no way to gather more data, you just guess. And often, you make mistakes.

In situations where you can't rationally find the answers you seek, your intuition is a powerful ally. Your intuition doesn't work in linear or analytical ways. It makes great leaps. It zigs and zags. It isn't possible to explain how you know what you intuitively know, but we have all experienced instances of getting intuitive hits that later proved to be accurate.

The problem with intuition is that it comes and goes. It isn't easily controlled, and it isn't consistent. When you are needing to make a health choice, it doesn't always offer you the answers to your questions. What if there were a way that you could use intuition in a focused way?

Well, there is. It's called dowsing, and it is a natural skill we all have. But for any number of reasons, it is not widely accepted or used in modern society. Dowsing is a way of getting answers to questions you cannot answer rationally. It is the perfect tool for the Healing Made Simple process.

With accurate answers to just about any health question, you can be more assured of success in your healing journey. Instead of trial and error and all the frustration and cost associated with it, you can use both your rational and intuitive minds in the appropriate ways to have faster, smoother healing.

This book is not a dowsing training guide. We recommend you avail yourself of the Chapter Thirteen - Resources listed in that section of the book if you want to pursue this natural human skill. For the purposes of this book, we will explain one method of dowsing that doesn't use a tool which you can learn fairly quickly, so you can get a taste of how powerful this natural knowing is.

What Is Dowsing?
First let's outline the basics of the skill of dowsing before teaching you a technique. If you visit a chiropractor, and he uses muscle testing on you, that is a type of dowsing. He is using your body to get answers to questions like, "Where is the misalignment?" Kinesiology is a form or subset of dowsing, and it is widely used and accepted as useful in healing practices.

Muscle testing and dowsing look pretty easy to learn. That's because getting a 'yes' or 'no' answer seems to be the hardest part. After all, it's the answers we are seeking, so once we are able to get those, we must be good to go, right?

Because dowsing is a skill, there is much more to it than that. You need to practice and learn key parts of technique in order to get accurate answers. First, you need to learn how to get into a dowsing state, which is a special, receptive state of mind that allows the accurate answers to come through. This is hard to describe, difficult to teach and a challenge to learn.

Next, you need to be able to form a very clear and specific dowsing question. Most people, including most dowsers, aren't very good at this, so their answers aren't worth much. They ask vague questions and get answers that aren't really useful. It takes time and practice to learn how to form good dowsing questions.

The next step is of course the dowsing itself and getting the answer, which most people are aware of. Your tool or body indicates a 'yes' or 'no' response. All dowsing questions are worded to be yes/no or true/false.

Finally, you need confirmation of your answers, because without that, you cannot improve. Your mistakes are actually a bigger potential learning experience than your successes if you use them to improve your technique.

There are many pitfalls beyond poor technique that can reduce your accuracy. It is beyond the scope of this book to go into detail on this subject, but it would be wise for you to use the Chapter Thirteen - Resources section to pursue masterful dowsing. So let's give you a basic training in The Body Sway so you can start getting answers.

The Body Sway

Probably the most favorite deviceless dowsing technique is the Body Sway. You don't need a tool to do it, and it's pretty hard to fake it. Your body becomes the indicator of 'yes' or 'no', and gravity and your body weight work against any tendency to cheat.

When you do this, start out in a quiet place by yourself. You don't want distractions, and you want to avoid skeptics. You'll need to get into a receptive state for the answers to come through.

Stand with your feet shoulder width apart. Stand straight, but relaxed. Empty your mind completely. Be curious. You are wondering what your body is going to do when you ask the question. Release any emotions. Don't think of this as a test.

You know where you were born. Even if you don't know the exact city, you know the state/province/country. So let's see what your body's 'yes' response is. You can pose this as a question or statement. You can say it out loud or to yourself.

The statement is, "I was born in_____(name the place) in this lifetime." 'Yes' or 'true' are the same body motion. For most people, they are a forward pull. Newbies often have to wait a while for the answer to come through. Be patient. And the answer may be weak at first. If you practice, it will get stronger and faster.

If your 'yes' is something different, don't worry. Just make a note of it. Now let's find your 'no' answer. 'No' and 'false' are the same body motion. Make a false statement like this, "I was born in _____(a place far from your birthplace) in this lifetime." Note what your body does. For most people, 'no' is backwards motion.

The important thing is that your 'yes' and 'no' be different, so you can tell one from the other.

There are pitfalls to avoid in dowsing, but this will give you the basics so you can get started. Use the Chapter Thirteen - Resources section to pursue dowsing mastery.

Use Your Whole Brain

Learning to use your intuition is showing your intention to use your whole brain and all of your senses. The rational mind uses the physical senses and is quite good at analysis. It tends to be linear and a bit slow, though. Your intuition is fast, nonlinear and uses intuitive senses. It is particularly good at sensing the invisible. People often refer to the left brain as your logical, scientific side and the right brain as your intuitive, creative side.

Another way of looking at this is your head does the thinking, the rational part, and your heart does the feeling, the intuitive part. No matter how you express the vast difference between rational and intuitive sensing, it is clear that if you use both in appropriate ways, you are using more of your natural abilities, and that should lead to better results on everything.

We like to say that adding focused intuition makes you more intelligent, because you can get so many more answers using intuition than you can when only using logic.

Neither method is innately superior. Contrary to what our culture says, intuition is just as valuable and powerful as the rational mind. The judgment on value belongs in a particular situation. There are things that are best discovered using your rational mind and things that are more easily discovered using your intuition in a focused way.

Using both faculties is a more natural human state. In Nature, the human used intuition to sense when danger was near. He didn't do an analysis or gather data or debate. He 'felt' danger near, and he acted the way he was guided in order to stay alive. This happened very quickly and was a nonlinear process. The rational aspects probably contributed to the growth of a body of facts and knowledge that could be passed on and taught.

Dowsing uses both faculties. The dowsing question requires you to use your rational abilities. The actual dowsing is an intuitive process. Unlike many intuitive, information-gathering processes that have been popularized during the "New Age", dowsing uses both sides of your brain. Most of the others rely mainly or solely on intuition, such as in channeling or tarot readings.

When you use dowsing, we urge you to only use it on things you cannot answer rationally or easily in other ways. Your rational mind can help you find something on Google. But when the answer isn't available through research or other left-brain ways, dowsing is the way to go.

If you try to dowse someone's phone number instead of looking it up in a directory, you are essentially mis-using your intuition. On the other hand, if you try to determine rationally whether your dog can recover from this latest illness, you stand quite a chance of guessing wrong, because guessing is what you are doing. The rational mind cannot answer that question.

So what we are proposing is not that you throw out science and rationality, but that you incorporate dowsing as focused intuition and use both in appropriate ways. When the rational mind can more easily give you the answers, use it. When it cannot, then use dowsing.

You will see your intelligence expand. You will have more and more useful answers and better outcomes simply by using all of the abilities you were born with.

Dowsing is a skill, not a psychic gift, so it does require training and practice to master. We advise you not to use it for important health questions until you have reached a proper level of mastery. Even then, always get a second or even a third opinion on any important question.

Don't be afraid of making mistakes, though. You make health choices every day. Sometimes you make the wrong choice. That is just part of being human. By incorporating your intuition appropriately into the process, you will reduce your mistakes radically. It will build your confidence and give you better results.

Learning to use your intuition in this way is another step towards self-empowerment in your healing process. It does take an investment of time and effort and even some money to master dowsing, but when you do so, you are saying that you are taking charge of your health. That you intend to take the guesswork out of your healing process.

Overcome Blocks To Intuition

The following suggestions are not something you can accomplish quickly or easily, but they will help you to create the proper environment for using your focused intuition successfully as a tool in your healing journey.

Release Negative Emotions

One of the greatest enemies of the accurate use of focused intuition is fear. Negative emotions can easily drown out the quiet voice of your intuition. So it's important that you learn to release fear and other negative emotions if you intend to tap into your intuition.

Releasing negative emotions like fear is a tall order. The Emotion Code is a simple technique that is a good starting place. But usually, you need to progress to other means for changing your perception of reality so that your reactions are less negative. You may have subconscious beliefs about this being an unsafe world or past life trauma that is affecting you in this life.

Don't focus on the things that are blocking you. Don't make a crusade out of clearing things that are holding you back. Spend a bit of time doing that with the intention of shifting energy into a more open and positive place.

Spend more of your time doing whatever is necessary to create happiness, contentment and harmony in your life. Put your intention and efforts into becoming the balanced, happy person you want to be. That will naturally release negative emotions and strengthen your Inner Voice.

Release Attachment

Attachment is caused by fear. It is also caused by the rational mind's unwillingness to let go and allow you to use your intuition. In order to use your intuition well, you need to release attachment of all kinds. Detachment is required for accuracy in health dowsing, as in any dowsing application. Detachment is not something you can easily train someone to have. You can describe it, but a person has to develop it herself.

The best way to picture detachment is a curious attitude. You are curious about the answer to your dowsing question. But you are not attached to getting a particular answer. Nor are you concerned about being 'wrong'. You care about knowing, but it is with a curious attitude. Nothing else. No other emotions.

If you feel yourself tensing up when you are dowsing about something, you probably aren't going to get an accurate answer, because that tense reaction is a sign you are attached in some way. If you feel calm and open instead, simply wondering what the answer is, that is detachment.

Don't get ahead of yourself. Don't imagine what you must do if the answer is this or that. That will set off negative emotions. You are not required to take any particular type of action based on the answer you get. You have the freedom to choose to act or not to act. Be totally in the moment and only focused on getting an accurate answer. You can decide what to do with it later on. Trust yourself to do whatever is appropriate.

In training yourself to be focused, calm, open and detached, you will also be transforming yourself into a more grounded and happy person. To use your intuition in a focused and masterful way, you will have to become more energetically balanced, grounded and coherent. The spinoffs of activating your natural intuitive senses are many.

How Do You Do It?
There are many tools for releasing emotions and attachment. We have successfully used EFT (Emotional Freedom Technique, or tapping) for many years, and we continue to see good results with it. The Emotion Code has sometimes given us great results, too. Practice whatever modality seems to be aimed at releasing negative emotions, old patterns and creating harmony and peace within you,

and you will be getting rid of blocks to your intuitive ability.

Developing Your Intuition

By now, you may be convinced that learning to use your natural intuitive abilities will aid you in your health goals. In a way, you are returning to a natural human state in which you acknowledge the body's natural healing process and support it by doing whatever you feel guided to do to restore the balance. Because your body doesn't lie, if you can listen to it, you know what to do.

If this now resonates with you, congratulate yourself. You've come a LONG way from where you were when you picked up this book. Maybe you were doing holistic and energy therapies then, or maybe you were totally conventional. But you now feel more empowered to take charge of your healing process. And that is the biggest single step you can take to reach your health goals. You don't have to act like you cannot possibly understand your health. We're not talking college degrees or science here. We are talking natural knowledge that all humans have access to. Your body and your health are something you are coded to 'know'. It's a survival issue.

We are not saying you will never need outside help. Of course you will. We are not saying you can magically restore your health without doing therapies or something to shift energy. We are saying that if you step up and into your power, you will address the process differently. Instead of blindly taking a drug because the doctor said to, you will ask questions. You will tune into your own intuition to check and see if it 'feels' right. In so doing, you will heal better and faster.

My mother was highly intuitive. I was a sickly child, and I benefited many times from her following her intuition over what the doctors said to do. She was the one who said no to corrective shoes for my 'trick' knees and also to the idea of removing bone from my jaw to correct an overbite. In hindsight, while those suggestions may (or may not) have been made with my health in mind, they were unnecessarily complex, dangerous or unpleasant. My mother was the one who said no to various unpleasant tests like bone marrow samples when my blood values were off the charts. The doctors had no idea what was wrong, and she drew the line at invasive or horrible procedures that offered no promise of success. In retrospect, her intuition was so right. It saved me a lot.

But it wasn't until much later in life that I realized I was intuitive, too. I always regarded my mother's abilities as freakish and psychic rather than natural. It seemed so rare. I now know that anyone can tap into their intuition, thus expanding their intelligence and improving their healing process.

You may be where I was when I started getting involved in my own healing journey as the pilot, not the passenger. I had used holistic methods and learned energy healing. I then came across dowsing and started tapping into my intuition. At first, I doubted that my intuition was powerful. I didn't think I was like my Mom. My Mom certainly was a natural. Yet we all have that ability. Many of us have repressed it or buried it completely. But it's still there.

How do you re-activate your natural intuition and tap into its power? For most of us, that is a process, not an event. It's not like a Reiki attunement. If you haven't been using your intuition, it's like weak muscles. You cannot make them strong overnight. But with proper exercise, you can become strong physically.

Look at your intuition as a set of muscles you haven't used much. In order to strengthen them, you must simply use them. That's all it takes. Dowsing is a great way to 'pump iron' intuitively. But any intuitive activity is useful. Draw a tarot card each day as an answer to your goals or intentions. Meditate to learn to clear your mind and just 'be'. Release your fears and doubts using EFT or The Emotion Code. When you get an intuitive hit or a dowsing answer, follow through. (Of course if the subject is life or death, get a second or third opinion first).

Nothing builds your intuition faster than using it, trusting it and confirming it. At first you won't want to trust. You will be overcome with doubts. That is natural. Trust anyway.

Don't overstep your level of competence, as that is a way of seeking defeat. Use your rational mind and choose when to follow through on intuition based on your level of experience and competence. Don't be afraid of making a mistake. You can learn from mistakes. You make them all the time. But don't court disaster. In other words, use your judgment.

As you become stronger and more confident, your level of competence increases. Continue to expand beyond your comfort zone a bit at a time. Celebrate your successes. Learn from your mistakes. Keep growing. Before you know it, you will have a number of wonderful examples to share about how your intuition is 'kicking in' more and more often. The bottom line is that to become more intuitive, you just need to practice being intuitive. There is no magical way someone can 'make' you intuitive. But you can tap into and re-activate your intuitive abilities simply by using them and learning to trust them.

CHAPTER SEVEN
Methods Don't Matter: Mindset Does

It's All In Your Head

It's alarming when the light dawns on you, as it does if you work on improving your health long enough and ask the right questions. After you've learned several healing methods and tried them all, you are faced with the fact that no healing method works for every problem. You knew that in the beginning, but somehow you lost track of it in your enthusiasm and optimism about each new healing modality. You told yourself that THIS method was going to be the one that worked.

Each time you said that, you believed it. You got some results, but not enough. So you felt you had two choices: quit or move on. Learn a better method. So that's what you did. But after a while, you begin to question the wisdom of that course of action. Any kind of progress is good, even incremental, but the amount of time, effort and money you have put into the process is by now exorbitant. Maybe you need to look at things in a new way. Well, join the crowd. That happened to us, too.

If you've been paying attention to the Law of Attraction principles of manifestation and the basics about energies, you have to admit that the world doesn't work the way you once thought it did. It is vastly different.

You now realize that what you have been chasing as if it is a brass ring is not outside of you. It's not something someone else can give you, nor is there a magic formula or pill for achieving your health goals. Your health is created more by your mindset and beliefs than by anything else you do.

Your approach to health is the number one contributing factor to your health. It's even more significant than what you eat and whether you are holistic or allopathic in your preferences.

So if you want to change your health in some fashion, you must change how you think of your health. You need to transform your beliefs about health. In other words, your attitude and approach need to change if you want different results than you've been getting.

We've already spoken about the need for clear goals and a picture of what health means to you. We've addressed the importance of taking responsibility for your health and not feeling like good health is something that just happens. And we've spoken about addressing root causes rather than treating symptoms.

These are examples of how creating good health starts with how you think about health, not just what you do. We've also stressed the importance of looking at healing as a journey, not a destination. We've pointed out that including intuition in your healing journey will improve your results.

When you adopt these attitudes, your approach will of necessity change dramatically. But what you probably haven't even considered is that by acknowledging that good health begins in your head, you will be changing your approach to life in general. This is going to have far greater ramifications than you ever guessed.

What's Your Mindset?

So what is your mindset about health at this time? Don't feel you are being tested. There are no right or wrong answers. You will evolve in how you regard healing as long as you stay open to becoming wiser and getting better results.

There are many paths for reaching your health goals. In this section, we will discuss some of the common aspects that might change as you decide to become more empowered and take charge of your healing process.

Answer the following questions. Write your answers down. Then in the next section, put them together to see how they predict your health situation and your success at reaching your goals.

1. Victim Or Victor?
What percentage of the time do you feel that bad health is something that 'happens' to you, that is beyond your control? 0% means you feel that health is not in any way accidental or beyond your control. 100% means you think that all health issues have no relationship with your beliefs or actions. Give any number between 0 and 100% that represents how you feel about this.

2. Symptoms: Fear Or Curiosity?
On a scale of 0 to 100%, what percent of the time do you react to symptoms in fear, as in, "I wonder if this headache means I have high blood pressure" or "I am afraid this skin thing is cancer."? 0% means you never react in fear to a symptom, no matter what, while 100% means you always have fear when you have a symptom.

3. Empowerment: Are You In Charge?
On a scale of 0 to 100%, what percent would you say you are in charge of your health outcomes, with 100% meaning you believe they are totally in your control?

* * *

4. What Do You Focus On? What's Wrong? Or What's Right?

On a scale of 0 to 100%, when you are thinking about your body, what percent of the time are you thinking about what's wrong? 0% is if you never are focused on faults, ailments and bad things. 100% means that all the time you are thinking about health, you are thinking about what is wrong with your health or body. Pick whatever % is right for you.

5. Is Health Outside of You? Does Your Body Have A Natural Healing Ability?

On a scale of 0 to 100%, with 100% meaning you are totally in agreement in all situations, how much do you agree with the statement, "All healing is self-healing."?

6. Is Health A Struggle Or A Natural State?

Using a scale of 0 to 100%, how much do you agree with the statement, "Experiencing good health is a struggle."? 0% means you believe good health is a natural state, while 100% means you think one must struggle to attain and keep good health. Pick the percentage that matches your beliefs.

7. Is The Earth A Dangerous Place?

On the same scale of 0 to 100% and related to your health, how much do you agree with the statement, "The earth is a dangerous place"? 100% means you totally feel earth is dangerous to your health. 0% means you feel earth enhances and supports your health.

8. Are You Proactive Or Reactive About Health?

What percentage of the time on a scale of 0 to 100% are you reactive to your health? In other words, if you wait to treat problems as they come up, you are 100% reactive. If you spend most or all of your time focusing on prevention, that is 0%. Pick the number that reflects your behavior.

9. Do You Believe Your Goals Are Attainable?

If you have done the exercise earlier in the book on health goals, at this time, on a scale of 0 to 100%, how attainable do you feel those goals are? Totally would be 100%.

10. Do You Have Support Or Seek It?

This is a simple yes/no question. Concerning your health, do you seek and/or have outside support? This includes time spent reading, studying, taking classes, asking experts for their opinions, sharing with others with the goal of gaining knowledge, participating in forums on health, etc.

11. Are You Learning Healing Modalities?

Another yes/no question. If you have even one modality that you have learned, the answer is 'yes'.

12. Do You Hang Out With People Who Complain About Health Or People Who Are Empowered?

The answer to this should be the one that is most descriptive of your current behavior. So write 'complain' or 'empowered'.

Now go to the next section to see how to interpret your answers.

How Your Viewpoint Creates Your Results

In the previous section you answered some questions that will help you to see where you are at in terms of your approach to health and the healing process. This section will interpret your answers. You will find that if you are doing any work towards shifting energy and seeing things in new ways, that if you come back and take this 'test' in 6-12 months, you will give vastly different answers. And you will find that if that is the case, you will also notice that your healing journey has become smoother and perhaps even more enjoyable.

Question 1: Victim or Victor?

We spoke of the value of releasing victim energy early in the book. Victim energy is most often expressed as the feeling or belief that you have no control over your health. If you feel that health is an accident, you are in victim mode. If you feel that health is a choice, then you are in victor mode.

Being in victor mode does not mean you have perfect health. It is a measure of your mindset. Being in victor mode is an alignment with success, while being in victim mode aligns with drama and failure. Most people are somewhere between 0 and 100%. It's hard not to feel like a victim sometimes. But the more you express victor energy, the better your health results will be.

The tricky bit about energies is you cannot do them on command. It's like saying to a depressed person, "Snap out of it!" In order to act like a victor, you must have victor energy and feel like a victor. This seems like a Catch-22 to us. But there are ways of accomplishing it. Affirmations done with a supplementary method to enhance results (like tapping) can help you align with victor energy regardless of how bad things are now. Tapping in general is useful for shifting energies and emotions. There are many ways you can start to practice feeling more like a victor and less like a victim. Be willing to take baby steps. Don't get discouraged.

* * *

The empowered answer is 0% or close to it.

Question 2: Symptoms: Fear or Curiosity?

There is a name people call you if your physical symptoms always lead to fear of terrible diseases and outcomes. They call you a hypochondriac. Yet, for those of us who have had major health collapses, especially when the doctors couldn't help us, it was natural to develop a fatalistic and negative outlook on health.

It is totally natural to have fear if you have a bad symptom that seems to indicate a major problem. It is not 'natural' to immediately think you have a brain tumor if you have a headache, or that you have cancer if you have an unexplained pain somewhere.

You won't be able to have a balanced and empowered outlook on health until you release a lot of fear. This is not a one-time deal. It is an ongoing process, especially for those of us who have lived with poor health for many years. But I can attest that it works.

I personally have used tapping therapies and The Emotion Code with success for this purpose, but use whatever gives you results. By releasing fear, you will find you are less likely to focus on negative outcomes, thus less likely to attract them, and that you will be able to hear your Inner Voice better. Be patient and allow yourself to improve on your own timetable.

The empowered answer is 0% or close to it.

Question 3: Empowerment: Are You In Charge?

Your new approach to health requires that you 'step into your power'. This is a New Age-y term that is hard to define. In this case, we mean that you accept responsibility for creating good health for yourself. We spoke of responsibility earlier in the book as something you shouldn't be afraid of. It isn't blame. It is simply the ability to respond. If you wish to create good health, you must have the ability to respond.

Many people 'give their power away' by thinking they cannot

respond. They ask the doctor to take that job. We believe that is putting too much on the doctor. The doctor is a consultant on your health, a health expert you value. But the doctor is not responsible for your health. If you don't believe it, ask her. No doctor will accept that responsibility.

Therefore, you must ask yourself if your doctor is not responsible for your health, who is? And the obvious answer is: you are.

This is what stepping into your power is. It is about acting as if you know that you and only you are responsible for your health.

Now, if you have suffered from a toxic heavy metal exposure or a reaction to a vaccination or something like that, you may be in victim mode and want to say you cannot be fully in charge of your health, because you cannot control those factors. However, if you regard empowerment not as controlling what others do, but what you do, you are 100% in charge.

You are responsible for reacting to what happens to you, not for things outside of you. If you get a heavy metal exposure and you choose to dwell in victim mode and feel totally incapable of responding, it is unlikely you will get the results you desire. On the other hand, the attitude that you can respond and find help and improve your health is far more likely to yield positive results.

The empowered answer in this case is 100% or close to it.

Question 4: What Do You Focus On? What's Wrong? Or What's Right?

Our culture is one of self-judgment. If you are a 'normal' person, you probably tend to spend more time thinking about what's wrong with your health than what's right. For most of us, if our body is functioning great, we are thinking of other things, but when it malfunctions, we focus on everything that has gone wrong.

You might find that when you have a terrible sore throat or headache, you ask yourself why you never think to be grateful when you don't have throat or head pain. It's so awful. But it's pain that seems to get our attention.

It's good that you respond to pain and other symptoms, as they are messages about imbalances and things you need to fix. But try to treat them like an unpleasant telegram. Look for the message, then find solutions. Focus on what you intend to create, not what is wrong. This attitude will take time and a lot of practice, but you will see better results as you improve on spending more of your time on your progress, your successes and gratitude about what is right with your health.

0% is the empowered answer, or close to it.

Question 5: Is Health Outside Of You? Does Your Body Have A Natural Healing Ability?
The conventional view of health is that you go to a doctor to get it. It's like a product. It's something outside of yourself. You are deficient in health, and an outside force, action or item is required to become healthy.

A more enlightened viewpoint, in our opinion, is that the body is an amazing living thing that has the ability to restore balance and health if given some support and time. For the millions of years that humans roamed the planet without any doctors, their biggest survival threats were death by predator, each other, childbirth and infection.

There really isn't much that a homeostatic mechanism can do about those harsh realities. But humans would not be around today if the human body did not have the ability to return to health when it is imbalanced.

"Modern medicine" uses drugs and surgery that are powerful, give pretty fast results and are unlike most of the remedies historically used to heal people. The techniques of modern medicine seemed miraculous, and in some ways, they are. But they come with much larger side effects than natural remedies. We have almost become addicted to instant healing medicines. We want our cough or headache to stop now. We don't trust that our body can restore balance given time and support. Always looking outward for health remedies causes you to doubt that your body knows how to be healthy on its own. Yet it does.

You have a choice how to view the healing process, as something separate and outside of you, or as a natural process that your body engages whenever needed.

The empowered answer is 100% or close to it.

Question #6: Is Health A Struggle Or A Natural State?

There is no right or wrong answer here. Your answer reveals your attitude towards health, and that will inform your actions. If you have been experiencing a lot of health challenges, you probably will feel like health is a struggle, even if you did not in the past. It is important to be aware of your attitude, because not only does that color your choices; it contributes to the reality you manifest.

If you can focus on the idea that good health is the natural state of the human body, and that you are merely doing what you can to support the natural balance and intelligence of your body, you will get better results than if you see yourself as a victim of bad health who must fight to get healthy.

The empowered answer is 0%

Question #7: Is The Earth A Dangerous Place?

We have observed that among those who consciously or subconsciously believe the earth is a dangerous place overall, there seems to be a greater incidence of ailments, especially allergies, digestive issues and immune system problems. You manifest what you believe, so it behooves you to try to start seeing the earth as a place that is safe for you. You can acknowledge that sometimes bad things happen, but in order to boost your healing process, you need to release negative beliefs and attitudes about being here on earth. They will hamper your healing process.

* * *

If you find that you want to cling to those attitudes, that you argue and justify your judgment of life on earth, we are willing to bet you have had some serious health challenges, and that you have a pattern of ailments throughout your life. Your life experience is colored by your beliefs. So the question is, "Would you rather be right or healthy?" You can't have both if you insist that earth is a dangerous place.

The empowered answer is 'no'.

Question #8: Are You Proactive Or Reactive About Health?

Reactive people are on the defensive. Whether you are reactive in health or life in general, a defensive stance is resistant to all kinds of change, positive and negative. You can't easily get healing if you are in a defensive posture. Especially if your defensive posture includes anxiety and fear, your health will suffer.

Being proactive requires you to think about your health goals, which most people haven't done. Having goals makes success more likely. Being proactive means you take steps to reach those goals. Focusing on your intentions and taking what you believe to be right action is one of the best ways of creating positive outcomes in all areas of your life.

The empowered answer is 'proactive'.

Question #9: Do You Believe Your Goals Are Attainable?

It's all well and good to have goals, but if you don't believe they are attainable, you won't succeed. You know if you consciously believe your goals can be reached. But you cannot know your subconscious just by thinking. Dowsing is a great way to reveal what your subconscious feels about your goals.

Use the Body Sway to ask if your subconscious currently believes your health goals (assuming you have them) are 100% attainable. You can substitute different numbers and phrases, such as 'more than 80% attainable'. Or you can just ask a simple yes/no question.

If at any level you do not believe your goals are possible to achieve, you will have trouble achieving them. So it's important to get your conscious and subconscious minds on board with your health goals.

The empowered answer is 100%.

Question #10: Do You Have Support Or Seek It?

This may seem to be a counterintuitive question. We have told you how important it is to believe in yourself, to take control of your healing process, and that is good advice. But it is important to recognize that everyone needs outside help at times. Being open to receiving information, advice and support is an important part of your healing journey.

Seeking help comes in the form of taking courses, going to webinars, reading books and asking for health advice from a qualified professional. That is actually taking control of your health.

The empowered answer is 'yes'.

Question #11: Are Your Learning Healing Modalities?

If you take charge of your health, you will want to have some tools in your toolkit. A healing modality is valuable. More than one is even better. You may be drawn to herbology (herbalism or botanical medicine), Reiki or tapping. Take courses in whatever method attracts you, as it is probably a good one for you. No one method does it all, so learning a few is actually a very good idea.

The empowered answer is 'yes'.

Question #12: Do You Hang Out With Complainers Or Empowered People?

It is said that your income will not vary much from that of your circle of friends. The same is true of your health. Birds of a feather do flock together. Like attracts like.

If you are complaining about your health, you are stuck in ill health. Complaining does not help you heal. It's natural to be frustrated from time to time, but take care that you do not spend time around complainers. It is a sign you are stuck. Instead, hang out with folks who talk about the latest success they've had or the new method they are getting results with.

The empowered answer is 'empowered people'.

Change Your Mind; Change Your Health

The previous sections have given you a glimpse of what you need to change in order to see improvement in your healing process. It should be clear to you now that your mindset is the single biggest determining factor in your health, and that by taking charge of it, you will improve your healing process.

Let's say you are in agreement that changing your attitude is a good goal. How do you do that? There is no one magic answer to that very good question. Often, spiritual seekers will be thrilled to have a new outlook revealed to them, but after you get done doing your victory dance, then you have to get down to the nitty gritty of making things happen. And while you agree you need to change your attitude, you aren't too clear on how to do that. At that point, many people just give up.

We live in a wonderful time that offers many powerful transformational methods. Whereas 50 years ago, you just had to do it yourself, now you can use one of any number of methods that have been shown to shift energy effectively. Tapping is a favorite of ours. The Emotion Code can give good results. Meditation is helpful.

You are unique person. What works for me may not work for you. Dowsing gives you the opportunity to evaluate methods for your goals. If you want to overcome a tendency to doubt your body's ability to heal, you can dowse how effective on a scale of 0 to 10 tapping would be for shifting that energy and aligning with belief. Or you can just ask a simple yes/no question about the method. (We suggest you take our dowsing courses to increase your accuracy, because it is beyond the scope of this book to teach you advanced dowsing techniques.)

Results matter. You can measure them. Do what gives you results.

Change is not necessarily easy, and it is rarely fast. While we all wish we could just flip a switch and be healthy, it doesn't work that way. It takes time, discipline and patience to get results. It took me several years to recover my health after it collapsed. I refused to give up, and by the time I finished, I was healthier than I had ever been. But it was not easy to see progress from day to day. I had to take the long view. I often would compare how I felt to how I had felt a year earlier. I would evaluate overall trends, like my digestion seeming to be better and not getting colds or flu much at all.

Sometimes it helps to make a list of the symptoms or things that tell you whether you are healthy. Low energy, pain of some kind, poor digestion, sinus problems are a few examples. List the most common symptoms you have that cause you to feel ill or just not healthy. Assign a number on a scale of 0 to 10 for how you are feeling now or how the week or month has been. Keep a record and compare the numbers. Have a clear picture of what the numbers mean. In addition to using the 0 to 10 scale of intensity, you can use the same scale for frequency.

It is important to be able to see progress. Another way you can measure progress is to list positive things you want to experience. You may wish to feel energetic throughout the entire day; have clear mental focus; digest your food well. You can likewise keep a measure of how you are doing with your positive goals. Sometimes it is necessary to take the long view in order to see progress.

One mistake people make when they seek health is to spend a lot of time doing a healing modality or searching for a supplement or remedy. When you put the majority of your efforts into 'outside' actions, your results will be slower than if you put the same amount of time into transforming your inner self: your beliefs and attitude.

Your health is a reflection of the inner you. So in order to change your health, you need to change yourself: your viewpoint, your attitude, your approach. If you want different results, you need to do something different, not just more of the same.

Too often people get caught up in learning therapy after therapy.

Sometimes they see incremental progress as they go along, but they tend to become frustrated, because it is costly of time, effort and money to learn and practice all those modalities. I know it was for me. If you have trod that path, try a new one. Use transformational methods to change yourself. That is the fastest route to change.

CHAPTER EIGHT
Intention Is Everything

The Placebo Effect

One definition of the placebo effect is:

> "A remarkable phenomenon in which a **placebo** -- a fake treatment, an inactive substance like sugar, distilled water, or saline solution -- can sometimes improve a patient's condition simply because the person has the expectation that it will be helpful."

In our opinion, the placebo effect is a window into the actual workings of the healing process. Up until now, we have argued that your mindset is the single biggest factor in how you experience health. Your mindset is what triggers the placebo effect.

Someone who is given a sugar pill, but who believes it is a cure for something that ails her, will in a significant number of cases, get good results. How can it possibly be so? A sugar pill is not a cure for anything. Yet over and over, studies have shown that the placebo response is significant.

An important aspect of the success of a placebo appears to be that the person 'believes' it is a cure. Belief is a complex subject. It appears to include more than just your conscious agreement with something, as in "I believe in God".

It would appear that all aspects of your being must believe in order to have true belief. For example, you may consciously believe that the pill the doctor gives you should work, but your subconscious may be doubting, based on a past experience you had that says the doctor isn't always right. You may not even be consciously aware of this. Remember, you cannot know what your subconscious believes by using your conscious mind.

Your body includes your subtle energy body, which has various layers and all sorts of input of which you aren't consciously aware. So while it is true that belief seems to be an on/off switch, it isn't really. For example: you may say you don't believe in voodoo, and yet, if someone puts a voodoo curse on you, in some cases it will still 'work'. Why is it that nonbelievers can be affected by such things? Obviously it is not a conscious belief. But there may be a subconscious belief or a past life experience that triggers the 'belief' reaction on some level.

Let's go back to the sugar pill given to subjects in the test study. These people are told the pill does such and such. They may not even know that some people are getting a sugar pill and others get the real deal. But do all participants have the same level of 'belief'? Obviously not.

Some are participating in the study for money or other compensation. Others are concerned about a health issue and have been invited to participate in hopes this will help them. There can be various backgrounds, doubts and motivations present.

When the participant takes the pill, her intentions, goals and focus will have an effect on the results. In some cases, that will mean that even if she got a sugar pill, she gets cured. This is a dramatic example of the power of focused intention. Don't you think it would be wise to harness this natural, no-side-effect process for your healing?

All Healing Is Self-Healing

We've mentioned before that all healing is self-healing, no matter how it appears to have happened. The body has a natural ability to heal, to restore its balance.

You can take a pill or do aromatherapy or Reiki, but whatever method you employed is simply facilitating your body's natural healing response. This is not to downplay the value of such tools and therapies, but to give credit where credit is due.

It is a natural human tendency to view your healing as a product of whatever method you apply or a gift from whatever healer you work with. It is not accurate, though, and that attitude is not only disempowering; it is incorrect. As someone who is now taking a more empowered approach to health, you need to acknowledge that your body is responsible for your healing, and that your mind and all of your energy has an effect on that process.

Intention is a vital part of that process. Intention is an aim, goal or plan. Without intention, whatever you choose to do is merely a ritual. You are doing it because you were told to do it; because you paid for it; because someone said it would work.

Intention is the focus in your process. You can shoot an arrow or a gun, but without aiming, you will almost never hit the target. You can go on a diet, but without a goal, it is unlikely you will stick to it. They say the road to hell is paved with good intentions. It might be more accurate to say that the road to hell is paved with a lack of intention.

Un-conscious living does not help you manifest your goals. First, you need goals, but then, you need to consciously focus on them. There's a lot of talk about living consciously these days. Most spiritual seekers regard that as a terrific goal. But it isn't an easy goal to reach. Living consciously is really, really hard to do. Most of what we do all day, we do on autopilot. Driving a car, doing the housework, doing a task at work are all usually done on autopilot, that is to say, un-consciously.

We tend to associate fear and panic with conscious living. Remember when you were first learning to drive? That was a conscious effort. It was scary remembering all the things you had to do. Now, you drive un-consciously and it's a breeze. The fact that in the early stages of learning a skill, we tend to be conscious and have focused intention almost certainly explains the phenomenon of 'beginner's luck'. The first time you do anything that you want to do well, you are more conscious, focused and 'intentional' than you are in the next few times you do it.

That kind of focus takes a lot of effort, and we tend to be lazy. We associate stress and effort with conscious living; either that, or boredom. The buddhists say, "Before enlightenment, chop wood, carry water. After enlightenment, chop wood, carry water." What does this say about enlightenment? That your life outwardly won't appear that different. You will be doing the same things, but how you do them will change. If you are focusing on chopping wood while you are chopping wood, instead of a million other things, you will be more likely to chop wood well. In any case, you will be living in the moment and consciously, which has many benefits. Intention, focus and conscious living are part of the process of enlightenment.

It is a real challenge to focus on what you are doing and have an intention for the outcome. Do you think about anything while taking your vitamins? Of course you do! But you're not thinking about how strong and healthy they are making you. You are thinking about what to cook for dinner or how to get enough money to buy that new car. Or maybe you're complaining about how large and hard-to-swallow that fish oil pill is. The vitamins are great, but without your conscious, focused intention, they won't do as much for you.

Earlier in this book we had you set your goals for health. We then showed you how to get useful information via your intuition using a process called dowsing. That information can help you understand the root causes of your issue and the best method for resolving your problems. The next step is to employ the solution using focused intention.

Your dowsing will have revealed what method is the most likely to give you the results you desire. Whatever the method: tapping, Reiki or crystals, it will be intention that guides the healing process. The modality you choose has an energetic frequency. You are using that frequency to help anchor your intention and goals, to help you stay conscious and focused on the results you wish to achieve. Which method tests as best will depend on your energy. That's why there is no one-size-fits-all healing method. The anchor that will best suit you must resonate with your energy.

You body's self-repair mechanism is 'kick-started' or 'boosted' by the modality you choose. We all need a little help at times, and that's what these methods do for our healing process. As mundane as it sounds, those lovely healing methods are not healing you. You are healing yourself with the facilitation and help of those healing methods. This is an important distinction that will affect your viewpoint and approach to the healing process.

The Difficulty Of Using Intention

If you've made it this far, you know that the new approach to healing that we promote involves

1. Becoming empowered; releasing victim energy; accepting responsibility
2. Taking charge of your health by making goals
3. Making conscious choices of what you believe will support those goals
4. Using your intuition and trusting it to help you become an active (proactive) partner in your healing process
5. Knowing that the body has an amazing 'intelligence' that has the ability to heal
6. Being aware that focused intention is the most powerful single element in the complex healing process
7. Utilizing 'anchors' for your intention by picking the best modality (frequency) for accelerating or kick-starting your body's healing process

Focused intention as the engine for success makes a lot of sense. And it sounds easy. But it is not. Remember, we pointed out that acting 'consciously' is no easy thing for most people. Even if you manage to stay conscious for one minute, by the next minute, you are usually back in un-conscious mode. Un-conscious is the default (energy-saving) mode for humans.

It's important not to judge or be angry about this fact. Don't blame yourself or feel deficient. It's just the way we are. By being aware of that fact, you can take measures to overcome it. Here are some tips:

1. Learn more than one modality, and don't use the same one over and over. Repetition leads to rote behavior, which loses the focused intention. Switching from one method to another will force you to be alert and focused, at least for a while.
2. Spend time on your healing process daily, and do so in a

quiet, undisturbed setting. Don't have the radio or TV going. Peace, quiet and tranquility are your allies. Making an almost sacred act of whatever healing work you do is part of maintaining consciousness and powering focused intention.

3.   Alter as many aspects of your healing process as you can: when you practice it; what you practice; where you practice. Mixing things up helps keep you present and conscious. You will find this challenging and tiring, especially at first. You won't be able to create a routine that you can follow by rote. Good!

4.   Monitor your results. Measuring progress is an important aspect of building confidence. The less doubt you have, the greater confidence, and the greater belief you have, the better your results will be.

5.   Regularly practice using focused intention. The more you practice, the better you will become.

Even if you do all of the above, you will still be plagued by challenges. It is really tough for a single person to power intention is a dramatic way. That is not necessarily the case for groups of people. In 'The Intention Experiment", Lynne McTaggart amply proves using scientific studies that intention does work for groups. Time and again, it has been shown that the power of group intention gives significantly different results to no intention at all.

Not surprisingly, the studies mostly refer to groups of people as opposed to individuals. Some studies have shown that individuals can power intention in a measurable way, but most of those which have been reported refer to yogis and expert meditators and proven healers and other types of individuals who are considered 'enlightened' or advanced way beyond normal humans. You or I are not considered capable of such activity.

This doesn't keep us from trying. Affirmations are a popular and well-known form of focused intention, and most people don't get very good results from them. There are now products that claim to overcome the problems inherent in affirmations, but we haven't seen anything that really works to dramatically boost the power of intention for an individual except through the investment of time and effort.

There are various factors, and probably many yet to be discovered, that affect your ability to successfully power intention. One that we like to talk about is your body's electromagnetic field. This is not your aura. It has to do with the strength of the fields generated by your brain and your heart. If these fields are weak (which they are in over 85% of humans), you will have great difficulty manifesting your desires, that is, powering your intention.

By strengthening your EM field, you improve your ability to power intention all by yourself. But that alone doesn't always make a huge difference. Your subconscious beliefs and past and present life trauma have a large effect on your ability to power your intentions, both overall and specifically. Working to clear subconscious beliefs that contradict your goals will also help you power your intention better.

Yet we have observed that it becomes a never-ending search or struggle for success. You learn one method or clear one type of block, and then you have to find and clear another, and another. And your success is only incremental. True results elude you. This is probably because most people have the attitude that good health and success involve a great struggle and a lot of work, and it's hard to ever reach the destination when you have those attitudes. It's like seeing yourself as a spiritual seeker. If you define yourself that way, you will probably never reach a destination, as a seeker must continue to seek.

It's the Law of Attraction once again. That tricky little bit of advice about aligning and allowing is so hard to put into practice. It sounds so reasonable, but it seems so tough to achieve. This of course illustrates that you have the attitude that struggle is necessary and you must earn what you get, or possibly that you don't deserve what you want. What you consciously want eludes you, because you find it impossible to believe all you have to do is get out of your own way. It sounds so right, but how do you accomplish it?

The simple answer is that you have to change your outlook. Just like we've said all along. True change comes from changing your beliefs, your outlook, your values. That is part of the adventure and excitement of the healing and personal growth journey. And once you begin to enjoy that journey, you have gone a long way towards allowing the good things you want.

Everything Works

Intention works, but it doesn't work the same way or equally well for everyone. We've shown that groups seem to have more success with intention than individuals. Because you are unique, your energetic frequency and the imbalances in your system are unique to you. You need to find a healing method that is the right 'frequency'.

In spite of the fact that there are no one-size-fits-all healing methods, and we all know that, we still keep searching for that magic bullet. We know it's not rational, but we keep hoping that the next method we learn will fix everything. But it doesn't.

All healing modalities work. They just don't work all the time for everyone on everything. You need to find the right vehicle to power your healing intentions. It's always your intention that gets the body's healing on track. As we noted before, a sugar pill can trigger healing, and we all know that isn't medicine or magical. It's all about intention.

It's beyond the scope of this book to examine everything that blocks you from focusing your intention successfully, but just knowing that this is something you need to address can help you get on the path to improvement. Here is a list of some of the factors that can cause you not to heal, especially in terms of focusing your intention:

1. If you have weak boundaries or a weak electromagnetic field, you may have difficulty powering and focusing your intention. This is because you are not able to separate yourself from the energies in your environment, and many of those energies resonate with helplessness, victimhood and failure.

2. The frequency of healing that you have chosen may not be appropriate for what you need. If you are very holistic in your approach, consulting with an allopathic doctor will set up a lot of conflicting energies. You need to find

professionals who respect your opinion and resonate with your beliefs in order to smooth the healing process.

3. You may have subconscious beliefs and present/past life trauma that makes it very difficult to 'step into your power' and take responsibility for your health. Working on those issues will ultimately improve your results in healing.

4. It's very difficult to know your life's purpose. You know what you would like to experience, but the health challenges you are meeting are part of your life's journey, and getting the message and working with them will help move you forward faster. Don't see yourself as broken or defective. Each experience is an opportunity. Find the opportunity.

5. Success often presents itself in a package we did not expect. Often, we overlook it, because we are filtering out anything that doesn't fit our expectations. Work hard to be open to success in any form. That will speed the healing process.

6. Divine timing is a vague concept that is hard to define. But it is real. Most of us are impatient to see outward change. That is normal, but we need to accept that our desired timetable does not always match up with what is possible or even appropriate. Trusting the Universe is harder than it sounds. But one thing about the healing journey is that it offers you many chances to learn to do that, and once you do learn, healing does get easier.

Exercise
How Do You Exercise Intention?
Answer the following questions, which are designed to get you thinking about how you apply intention in your healing process. It will help you see how coherent and conscious your approach is, so that you can make changes to improve your results.

1. What methods of healing do you use most often at this time? Are they energy modalities? Supplements? Herbs and other physical methods? Therapies that turn to professionals, like chiropractic? Allopathic methods?
Make a list and look it over. Ask yourself why you pick the things you use. Do they all represent an empowered choice, or do some of them come from fear? Do you turn to professionals because you trust them and respect and believe in their methods, or because you feel incompetent to deal with things yourself? Do you find that the professionals you choose support your empowerment, or treat you as inconsequential in the healing process?

Make a note of the dissonant items on your list. How can you alter them, replacing them with something that is more empowering or even removing them, with the goal of improving your healing process and making it more coherent and smoother?

How many of the choices you make are determined by outside pressure as opposed to independent, conscious choices by you? The more you are choosing consciously, the better your results will be. (Of course that assumes your conscious choices are empowering and not self-sabotaging.)

2. Now that you understand the concept of 'anchoring' your intention, what types of anchors most resonate with you? Make a list.
Possible answers include, but are not limited to, supplements, herbs, oils, energy healing, tapping, The Emotion Code, prescription drugs,

surgery, counseling, energy clearing, detoxification, symbols, colors, sound.

This question will help point you at anchors that resonate with your energy at this time. That is important. The more you resonate with an anchor, the better. You may change over time, and that's ok. What resonates now won't necessarily always resonate. Update your list and go with what feels right. Better yet, dowse the effectiveness of whatever you feel drawn to.

3. What have you done to strengthen the power of your intention?
Have you worked on boundaries? Have you strengthened your body's EM field? Do you use energetic protection? Do you practice conscious living? What are the things you have done that lead you to believe you are improving your ability to focus and power your intention? How about making more time for them?

CHAPTER NINE
Get Outside Help As Needed

How To Know

One of the biggest, if not THE biggest, stresses in terms of your health is knowing when to get outside help. Everyone knows when they MUST go to the Emergency Room. It's obvious. They are bleeding profusely with bone sticking out their skin or some other obviously serious or life-threatening condition.

You know when you absolutely must get outside help. You are also pretty comfortable knowing those times when you can fix things yourself or they just aren't going to become serious enough for going to a doctor. Sniffles during allergy season or the headache from stress or dehydration don't need medical care, and you know it. You have an over-the-counter or home remedy that works fine for those things.

But in between the situations that send you to the ER or doctor and those which you take in stride without doing anything much is a continuum of 'gray area'. The gray area consists of times when you just aren't sure what to do. Maybe the symptoms aren't that bad, but they persist longer than you feel is appropriate for a minor problem. Or the symptoms are unpleasant, but not quite enough to jump into the car and drive to the ER or make a doctor's appointment.

What do you do when you are in the gray zone? Do you have a protocol? Some people might wait at least 3 days if they have a questionable symptom, just to see if it will resolve on its own. You might even choose to wait longer, for example, when you have a low-grade virus. Perhaps part of your protocol is to use your best all-purpose remedy during that waiting time and see if the symptoms abate. You might even tune into your intuition to try and get a feel for whether this is something you need to get professional help for.

But all of that is very vague and uncertain.

Whether you have a protocol for making your decision or not, you are merely guessing based on your past experience. And guessing is risky. Even educated guesses are often wrong, because they make assumptions that can be incorrect from the start. Every day you wait could be critical. Especially if your situation is due to some trauma or an infection. You aren't sure if the bone is broken, and you've heard that if you aren't sure, it probably isn't broken. Or the fever isn't that high, but it's hanging on, and you have other symptoms that distress you. If you guess wrong, you could have permanent damage or even die. The anxiety is exacerbated when the person suffering is your child or a beloved pet. They can't always tell you exactly how they feel, leaving you worried that you are doing the right thing by them. Being laid back and having positive expectations isn't always the way to go.

At the other end of the spectrum are the worriers who go to the vet or doctor or even the ER with things like the sniffles. These people feel they are 'better safe than sorry', and especially if they have insurance, they figure, why not use it? They fear not making the right decision, and 'free' health care seems to make it smart to double check just in case. Unfortunately, the cost of health care has skyrocketed due to frivolous demands being made on the system, which isn't flexible even under the best conditions. The weight of caring for people who aren't really sick has led to incredible cost increases.

The point is, you can guess wrong. You can hold back when you should be rushing to the ER or doctor, leading to serious health consequences, or you can go to the ER or doctor when you have no need whatsoever, clogging up the system. This is the problem with the gray zone. You are just guessing. You will either be overly conservative or too confident that things will be ok. Either way costs you.

So back to where we began. Perhaps one of the greatest benefits of the Healing Made Simple approach is the use of dowsing to determine whether or not you would benefit from going to the doctor or ER. Here's the thing: you are going to decide one way or another. Dowsing just makes it easier to get an accurate answer, assuming you have been practicing your technique and are an accurate health dowser.

Dowsing is not 100% accurate. Nothing is. Guessing, even educated guessing, is only somewhat better than tossing a coin. Although it's true that your dowsing can be wrong, we have found it to be amazingly accurate for our needs. Granted, we are expert health dowsers. We also independently dowse, so each decision has at least two expert dowsers weighing in. You would be wise to get a good dowsing buddy, practice your technique and always get a second opinion like we do. But the bottom line is, you will make a decision. Use everything in your power to make it a good one.

We have argued about the value of including your intuition and gut feelings in the healing journey. Dowsing focuses your intuition and helps you cut right to the chase. Our experience is that we make far more good and accurate choices since we started dowsing in the gray zone. Honestly, I cannot remember even one choice that we regret.

I have to admit that especially for our pets, I fit into the 'worrier' camp. I would in the past far rather spend the time, effort and money to take an animal to the vet than to take a chance on him or her dying. Since we have been dowsing about that choice, we have saved literally thousands of dollars in vet bills by not wasting time, effort and money on unnecessary trips to the vet. (When you have 12 pets, it's pretty easy to rack up the savings.)

If we are talking about human health care, those of you who favor holistic treatment are probably paying out of pocket for most of it. You can save a lot of money using this method, because you won't be out of pocket for things you don't need.

For those who are in the current, conventional health care system, some processes still cost you money, and they all cost you time and effort. Taking time off from work, driving to an appointment and going through a lot of tests isn't something you want to do if you don't benefit from it. So even if it costs you no money, it's still a waste to go in when you aren't needing outside help.

How To Determine When You Need Help

So how do you know when to ask for help? That's the million dollar question. In this chapter, we're going to show you the procedure we use.

It won't do you any good at all unless you are an accurate, confident dowser. Don't even think about doing this unless you are sure you are a good dowser. Go back and practice your technique and develop confidence and proven accuracy, and then return to this chapter.

You're still there? OK. Here's the basic procedure, step by step (read further for details on each step):

1. Get into a dowsing state.
2. Ask your programmed dowsing question. (An explanation follows; see Step 2 below)
3. Note your answer.
4. Get a second opinion from a dowser you trust, or ask for a conventional opinion from another source.
5. Tune in to your intuition/heart and feel whether this answer seems 'right' to you.
6. Take appropriate action.
7. Over a reasonable period of time, continue to monitor the situation and dowse again as needed to verify that things have not changed and do not require different action.
8. If you feel that your answer was incorrect in retrospect, go back and look at your procedure and find out where you went 'wrong'. Work on eliminating that problem for the future.

Never do this unless you are an accurate dowser, and always get a second or even a third opinion. If your answer feels 'wrong', go with your gut and do whatever feels

'right'. **Never use your own dowsing to decide about life or death situations. Get outside help.**

Step 1: The Dowsing State

We have observed that most dowsing training is deficient, in that it often doesn't even mention the dowsing state, which is a critical part of the dowsing process. If you are not in a dowsing state, you are not dowsing. Please see the Chapter Thirteen - Resources section if you need dowsing training. We offer many types for all levels of experience.

The dowsing state is the proper mindset to allow the answer to come through to you. You need to have a curious attitude when dowsing. You must not be fearful, nor can you be attached to getting a certain answer. If you are emotional or attached, do not dowse. Practice is the only way to learn the proper degree of detachment for dowsing about important subjects.

A proper dowsing state is curious, calm, emotionally unattached and open and clear to receiving the answer to your question.

Step 2: Your Dowsing Question

We prefer to use a technique called 'programming' to make it easier to get an answer when times are stressful. Most people aren't going to easily be able to remember all their priorities when they are in a crunch to decide about whether to go to the vet or ER or not.

So when things are calm one day, make a list of all the situations that would make you want to get a 'yes' answer to the question, "Should I go to the vet/ER/doctor for this situation?" You are unique. Your needs and preferences are unique. You need to customize your question so that your answer best reflects your values.

Some things on your list might be:
- Give me a 'yes' if this is a life-threatening condition
- Give me a 'yes' if I don't have the tools or experience to resolve it on my own in a timely, safe and satisfactory way
- Give me a 'yes' if the doctor/ER/vet will be able to resolve

this faster/better/with fewer side effects than if I treat it myself
- Give me a 'yes' if whatever the doctor/vet will recommend is within my budget of $_____/is covered by my insurance/is something I would be able and willing to agree to do

You get the picture. Your financial needs, personal preferences and experience will dictate under what circumstances you will want to be sure to be directed to seek outside help, and under what circumstances you would prefer to not invest in outside assistance.

Some people won't include money as a factor (lucky them), but if money is a factor, you need to include it. Others might consider time an important factor, because they don't get paid sick leave to go to a doctor. Write down as many of your preferences as you can think of. Be sure to revise it over time. Add to it. Change it as needed.

Now make your programmed question. It should be a simple question that takes everything on your list into account. Ours is, "Should I go to the vet/doctor/ER for this situation?" Those of you who follow us will recall that we say never to use the word 'should' in a dowsing question. It implies obligation, which is not a factor you want to introduce into your dowsing. In this case, however, you will set your intention that whenever you ask the programmed question, what it really means is a long question that takes your entire list into account.

Here's an example of how to 'program' your question, but you must make your question customized. **This is for demonstration purposes only.**

Get into a quiet space and have your list and question written out in front of you. Then set your intention and speak it out loud. "Whenever I ask the question, 'Should I go to the vet/doctor/ER with this problem?', please give me the answer to this longer question, and make it 'yes' if any of the following are true: "Is one of the following true: this is a life-threatening condition/I don't have the tools or experience to resolve this in a safe and timely fashion without outside help; the doctor/vet/ER will resolve this faster/better/with fewer side effects than if I treat it myself; whatever the doctor/vet/ER recommends as further action is within my budget of $_____ and is something I would be willing/agreeable to do."

You can see how hard it would be to remember all these factors in a crunch, and how easy it is to have a shorter, simpler question to ask that represents the longer question you have written out.

Step 3: Your Answer
Get your dowsing answer.

Step 4: Get A Second Opinion
Have another dowser also dowse the question. Or ask someone to use another method, such as logic, to render an opinion on what action is in your best interests. Make sure that whomever you consult is not answering based on emotions like fear and worry, and that their values are aligned with yours.

Step 5: Tune In
Take the time to listen to your heart. How does your answer feel? If it feels 'wrong', you need to do what feels 'right'. If you are merely feeling resistance, fear or doubt, that is normal, even when you are not dowsing. Use your best judgment as to what to do.

Step 6: Take Action
Make a decision and take action. You were going to, anyway. You were going to guess, and guessing isn't accurate. There are no guarantees at times like this. Take the best action you can.

Step 7: Keep Asking
In many situations that arise in the 'gray zone', you may make a decision not to take action, but that doesn't mean you should quit asking. Determine what the best schedule is for your condition, and ask regularly if things have changed. Once or twice a day is usually good, except in acute situations, which might benefit from asking

every hour or so.

Continue to consult your intuition through dowsing until the situation is resolved. Don't be afraid to accept a different answer than you got yesterday, but don't keep asking the same question over and over at the same time, because doing that will nullify your answers.

Step 8: Review Your Results & Improve Your Procedure
No process is 100%. Guessing is only 50/50. Educated guessing with a bit of intuition is better. Dowsing improves your odds tremendously IF YOU ARE A COMPETENT DOWSER. That is a big 'if'.

When the inevitable mistake occurs (and it will), look at what you did and try to determine how you can improve your technique or procedure for the future. Mistakes are a great learning experience if you use them properly.

If the above procedure seems to long and complex, that's just because you haven't implemented or practiced it. It's actually very fast once you have all the parts in place.

CHAPTER TEN
Prevention

The Emphasis On Prevention

It's obvious that the new approach to healing we are proposing is more in alignment with natural, gentle, holistic, energetic methods. That doesn't mean you cannot apply the principles if you are in an allopathic mindset. You can still apply many of the principles. It's just easier with a more natural and metaphysical approach.

Prevention is an obvious next step in this process, which of course is also more in alignment with a holistic viewpoint. It makes far more sense to head off health problems than to try and fix them, especially once they become entrenched. Whether you view the world as we do and regard health issues as starting in the energy body, or you think they are purely physical, you have probably noticed that longstanding issues are harder to fix as a rule.

Prevention can be expensive. It requires a greater level of consciousness; a greater commitment; a bigger up front investment of time, effort and money in order to create the results you desire. To many people, who have come to regard free health care as an entitlement to get 'fixed' regardless of their lifestyle choices, prevention is a non-starter. But if you have stepping into an empowered place and want to co-create good health, prevention is a no-brainer. And you realize that although it requires an investment, it isn't any harder than having to deal with cancer or some other degenerative disease that robs you of happiness and health. In the end, it costs you no more than the old approach, and it gives you more years of happy, healthy living.

Implementing prevention in whatever form fits your beliefs is an important part of taking charge of your health. By acting preventively, you are saying that you believe that what you do has an impact on your health. You are saying that you believe that if you take charge, you can create the health you want.

It is important to differentiate between preventive measures taken due to a positive attitude and those taken out of fear. For example, testing has become more prevalent in recent years for certain genetic dis-ease markers. People are being scared into getting tested and taking action as if they are already broken, when they have no signs of dis-ease. Women allowing their breasts to be removed preventively is one example of this. Breast cancer doesn't occur because you have breasts. It doesn't occur just because you have a certain gene. Not everyone gets breast cancer, because it is a complex situation. We believe energy, emotions and various other factors are actually highly significant, and you can do something about those things.

Many metaphysical people have long felt that too much emphasis is placed on genes and DNA as if they cannot be changed. In past years, we were laughed at for believing in the plasticity of genetic expression. In recent years, epigenetics has become a hot topic. Even scientists now believe that there is more flexibility in the expression of DNA and genes than was formerly known. We believe you actually have a good deal of control over those factors, and our approach helps you to exercise that control to create more positive outcomes.

Your energy and your emotions and your beliefs are what matter when creating health. If you act out of fear, having a sense of doom and powerlessness, you will not get the results you would get if you act in an empowered way, believing that you can create health by taking certain actions.

So prevention can take two forms: empowered or fear-driven. If you are acting out of fear, prevention is not that helpful. Every action you take will work towards creating that which you fear instead of what you desire. Your intention is vital. Be aware of your intention when you take preventive action. Be sure you are focused on creating positive health, not on overcoming or avoiding something negative.

* * *

This highlights the critical nature of being honest with yourself and working on your own issues and attitudes and beliefs about health. Creating your healthiest life is not so much about the actions you take, but about the emotions, beliefs and intentions behind those actions.

One of the biggest preventive things you can do for your health is to release fear and to really start believing that you have the ability to create the health you want. We're right back where we started. If you see yourself as a powerless victim, you won't get the results you want. Your healing journey will be much smoother and more successful if you do whatever it takes to shift your energy into empowered and positive mode.

There are many ways to accomplish this. Belief clearing, emotional release, affirmations: don't just pick one method. Do a variety of things to shift your energy into the place of allowing good health, believing in good health.

Learn to observe how you feel and be honest about it. Let your emotions guide you. Don't judge yourself if you still have doubts or fears. You will never get rid of all of them. Be grateful that you have the ability to transform energy and align yourself with your goals. Be willing to adapt your actions to reflect changes. Don't keep using one method over and over long past its ability to give you success. Remember, healing is a journey, and along the way, you will be exposed to many opportunities for shifting how you think, feel and see life. Try to enjoy them.

Exercise
The Importance of Self-Awareness
In this exercise, you will be asked to answer a few questions. Notice not only your answers, but how your answers make you feel. Notice what you think about when answering the questions.

Be open to admitting you are fearful or negative. It is normal. Do not judge yourself. Only by becoming aware can you then take steps to make changes. Any changes you make should not be based on self-judgment. They should be founded on the desire to see things in a new way, because you are convinced that doing so will improve your health.

1. Make a list of the preventive actions you are currently taking. Include pills, supplements, therapies, etc.
For each item, tune into your core reason for using it. Why are you doing it? Are you afraid that if you stop, you will get sick? Do you feel dependent on that method/supplement? Do you have a lot of negative feelings about the expense? What negative thoughts come to mind?

For any item that you find you have negative feelings and thoughts about, write down what those are. This is a good opportunity to get to know yourself better.

Can you trace your feelings or beliefs to an event or person you know? Your childhood or family patterns? Beliefs you've developed or were programmed for? Use tapping, The Emotion Code or another method to help shift those energies.

Don't stop any important medication or therapy, but if you really do not believe in something and feel very negative about it, you need to speak with whomever recommended it and find a way to shift your attitude so you can get better results. In some cases, that might even mean no longer using the supplement or remedy.

Go very carefully and make all decisions with your health care professional's advice, but also learn to listen to your intuition.

2. How much do you believe on a scale of 0 to 100% that each method or remedy is significantly contributing to your healing process and the creation of good health for you?
Are you taking pills just because the doctor says so? Do you let the chiropractor tell you what supplements to use, even though you are not convinced they work?

Remember that intention is vital, and if you don't believe that what you are doing will help you, it probably won't work that well. Do whatever it takes to get committed to whatever methods and processes you are doing.

Remember the placebo effect. Your goal should be to align with being able to have healing be that easy.

CHAPTER ELEVEN
The Healing Journey

Your Healing Journey

People like to use analogies about healing. They say healing occurs in layers, and it's like peeling an onion. Or they say healing is a journey, not a destination. You may have been programmed to say or even accept this viewpoint, but deep down inside you have to admit: you want things to change fast. You want results NOW.

If you consider yourself a spiritual seeker, you might use this impatience you feel as a sign that there's still a lot of work to be done before you are enlightened. If you are judgmental, you may use your impatience as an excuse to feel deficient. Maybe you aren't even aware of your impatience. But it's there.

We've worked with a lot of clients over the years. We've worked on ourselves. It's rare to find anyone who feels patient and comfortable when they are having unpleasant physical symptoms. The longer you have the symptoms and the worse they are, the more you judge yourself to be defective or broken, and the harder it is to picture yourself as able to be healthy, let alone as healed.

These unfortunate attitudes will make your healing process unbearable. They are the results of a conventional mindset that says if you have a symptom, there ought to be a pill to erase it. We live in a culture of instant gratification. We think science can fix anything, notwithstanding facts to the contrary.

For the first time in written history, humans are raised to believe that their health is someone else's job. That if they get ill, they are not responsible in any way, and that they should be able to expect free treatment with the fanciest techniques and drugs available. People have learned to expect no consequences from bad habits or lifestyle choices. Instead, they focus on fixing things when they break. Perhaps this attitude began way back when science started regarding the body as a machine…

You can't really see healing as a journey if you have that perspective. And you can't expect to change that outlook overnight or simply by wanting to change. You are at a crossroads. You have been presented with a whole new way of thinking about health. It doesn't mesh with the old way at all. We've led you through the process of how to adopt this new approach to healing. But this is where we tell you it takes time to make this shift.

You may already have been drawn to this new way of looking at things. You may 'know' in your heart that it is the way for you to go. Even if you are resonating with it strongly, you still have many habits to break. You need to train yourself to see things in new ways.

If you just paste this approach on top of your old approach, not only will it not help you, it could hinder your healing process. The two contradict each other in fundamental ways. You are being asked to change how you see things, how you approach things. You need time to think about the implications and ramifications of this in your life.

For instance, you may find that if you adopt dowsing and start acting more empowered in your healing process, that your doctor will be offended. Many doctors are authoritarian. They want to issue orders with few explanations and no input from you. If you find yourself in this situation, you will need to make a choice. Do you continue to let the doctor make all your decisions, or do you find a new doctor who will encourage your participation, even appreciate it?

It surprises us the number of people who believe in the approach we describe in this book who report to us that their doctor would never believe in dowsing, nor welcome their input. Or that they are afraid to offer their opinion to their doctor.

There are great doctors out there. Don't let your participation in a particular health insurance model or your natural shyness prevent you from doing what you know is right for your health. Courage is required to take right action sometimes.

Your health is your most precious possession. You need to take care of it, not ask someone else to. No one cares more about the condition of your health than you do.

Your Healing Team

Part of the journey is putting together your healing team. When you take over control of your health, it's up to you to find people to work with whom you feel comfortable with, and whom you would like to see as members of your team.

Your health needs are unique. You may benefit from a chiropractor or an acupuncturist. Maybe you need a heart specialist. Whatever you determine you need, don't sit back and let someone else choose your team without your input. Choose conventional or holistic. Do research online and ask experts what they suggest. Include energy treatments and physical support.

Be open to having your team evolve as you change. You may not always need monthly chiropractic or weekly massage, and hopefully, if you are on a drug, you can plan to wean yourself off of it at some future date when your healing is complete. Never see yourself as stuck where you are now.

It is not rude for you to move on to other professionals as your needs change. Don't allow yourself to make your choices personal. You merely are doing what you think is best for your health. Always listen to your heart and go with what you are guided to do. Use dowsing to help you make good choices that will be more likely to help you reach your health goals. (If this is hard for you, if you tend to hate hurting people's feelings, this is an opportunity for you to create better boundaries and put your needs first. Do it.)

Be appreciative of your team. Express yourself, ask your questions and be open about your concerns. Be sure your team resonates with your energy and values. (If you are painfully shy about expressing yourself, that is the opportunity here. Take advantage of it.)

Include a spiritual component to your healing team. Within your own belief system, ask for help from whomever you picture as able to assist you on a spiritual level. You might ask your angels or guides or even the fairies to help you in your healing journey. Or you may ask for help within the bounds of a traditional religious tradition using prayer. This request for outside assistance of a spiritual nature is very helpful in your healing process.

Inner Change

Setting up your healing team is great and actually easier to do than the inner work required for success. If you never go beyond putting together a crack healing team, you won't see optimal results. So let's talk about the really hard part: changing yourself and your perception of healing.

We've spent a good part of this book suggesting things that you would benefit from changing. But how do you do that? What's the best way to: focus on what you want; take your power back; be patient and know that healing is a journey, not a destination?

If you've made it this far (congratulations!), you are committed to healing. And you just wish someone would give you a list of things to do so you can get on with it. But it is never that easy. If it were that easy, more people would be healthy, and it would have come to light that there is one perfect way to attain health.

Unfortunately, that is never going to happen. The beautiful things that make you unique also mean that your healing journey will be unique, as well as your blocks or challenges. It's up to you to overcome them, and no one can give you an easy formula for that.

When we refer to the healing journey, we aren't even referring to just 'curing' one problem, even a longstanding one. We are talking about living a healthy life. It's a matter of shifting focus from what is wrong in your life to what you want to experience. And that seems to take a massive amount of effort.

Healing is first and foremost about personal growth. In fact, to us, it is a subset of personal growth. Your health is about your viewpoint; how you react to the world; how you express the accumulated energies of this and other lives; how much you value yourself; how you express your creativity and so much more. So it comes down to change yourself to change your health.

We recommend reference guides in the Chapter Thirteen - Resources section that will help you get started at looking at the basis of good health. Next, you need to put together your tool kit for personal growth. What methods work best for you to shift your perception, beliefs and behaviors? We favor tapping of all kinds and have used it for many years with great results. Of all the many healing methods we have learned, it remains a valuable and effective tool for change. But that might not work well for you.

We recommend that instead of looking for a 'healing' method, you look for a method that shifts energies within you, that helps you shift your perceptions, beliefs and emotions. This is the key to faster, better healing in our opinion.

Watch for results. Practice and become good at your chosen method. Measure results. After you have given it a fair amount of time, if you haven't seen results, move on to another method. (Don't become like a bee flitting from flower to flower, though. Really give yourself time to master and see change before moving on to another method.)

When you find a method you like, practice it daily. Note that you won't find one method that does it all. Keep looking for other ways of shifting the energies that your favorite method doesn't handle well. Even simple things like colors, crystals, sound and symbols can be powerful tools for change.

Notice as time passes and you learn all these methods and shift a lot of energy, that you become a whole different person. You will see progress with your health, but even more, you will realize you are vastly different from the person who got sick. Good! That's what you should be aiming to see.

In addition to learning methods, which are tools, study how to change your perception. We have found the Law of Attraction to be powerful in terms of looking at yourself, the world and your ability to manifest outcomes in new, more empowered ways.

Get Support
Having a safety net or support group is helpful for smooth change in your healing process. Don't hang around people who complain all the time; find a group of positive people who will support your healing journey and are willing to be your cheerleaders. There are many in person and online groups that you can use. Going it alone is usually harder than having like-minded people to share your journey.

Each person is unique, but there is a great benefit to hanging out with like-minded folks. When you are down, they can lift you up and encourage you. They can share experiences and offer suggestions. While being part of a group may not fit everyone's healing journey, it is beneficial for most people.

Simple Does Not Equal Easy
Simple is not the same as easy or quick. We've given you a more simplified way of looking at the big picture of your health. That doesn't guarantee specific results. It certainly doesn't mean you won't have to work. You will still have to invest time and effort and even money on your health. This approach is about making your path smoother, more rewarding and maybe even at some point, happier. But don't expect overnight change. Have positive but realistic expectations.

It Takes Time
The process of shifting into a more empowered perspective and learning to manifest positive outcomes and believe in yourself is a slow process for most people. Each day provides opportunities for learning gratitude for the here and now, as well as empowerment to

create positive health outcomes.

The more you learn to be grateful and live in the present, the better the present looks. And the more you enjoy the life you have at this moment, the happier your life becomes, and the more happiness you attract, since like attracts like.

The health you desire will come not from hating who you are and what you are now experiencing. It will grow out of gratitude and joy in the present moment, loving the person you now are and being open to the future unfolding as it will, knowing you will have a fulfilling and happy life. This change in your perspective will make the journey a joy.

CHAPTER TWELVE
What Next?

Recommendations & Request
Please Leave A Review
We request that you leave an honest review of this book on Amazon so that others may make a good decision about buying it. The more detailed your review, the more help it will give others.

If you didn't like this book, have requests or suggestions for making it better or just want to contact us and tell us you loved it, write us at support@discoveringdowsing.com.

Learn To Dowse
Dowsing is a skill that takes time, practice and guidance to master. We would love to teach you to dowse accurately. For some free help, visit https://dowsing.leadpages.co/free-dowsing-instruction/

Dive Deeper Into Healing Made Simple
If you enjoyed this book, we recommend our online course "Healing Made Simple" for taking it to the next level. Details here: http://thesixthsensesolution.com/courses-and-replays/healing-made-simple-course-details/
For $30 off, use the coupon code 'simple' (without quotes) while checking out.

CHAPTER THIRTEEN
Resources

Books, Websites & Courses
Books For Deciphering Messages From Your Body
"You Can Heal Your Life" by Louise Hay

"Feelings Buried Alive Never Die" by Karol Truman

"Messages From The Body" by Michael J. Lincoln

-

Learn To Dowse
Dowsing is a skill that takes time, practice and guidance to master. We would love to teach you to dowse accurately. For some free help, visit https://dowsing.leadpages.co/free-dowsing-instruction/

Join The Dowsing Tribe
Free videos, replays, audios, articles and forums at the Discovering Dowsing website, http://discoveringdowsing.com.

Dowsing Products
Visit The Dowsing Store for courses, articles and events. http://thesixthsensesolution.com/shop/.

Dowsing Services
Want someone to dowse for you? Visit our website and browse our services. http://sixthsenseconsulting.com.

-

Dive Deeper Into Healing Made Simple
If you enjoyed this book, we recommend our online course "Healing Made Simple" for taking it to the next level. Details here: http://thesixthsensesolution.com/courses-and-replays/healing-made-simple-course-details/
For $30 off, use the coupon code 'simple' (without quotes) while checking out.

-

Methods We Recommend For Shifting Perception & Energy

Tapping methods like EFT (Emotional Freedom Technique)

The Law of Attraction

The Emotion Code

47092871R00074

Made in the USA
Charleston, SC
28 September 2015